MACHINE
EMBROIDERY

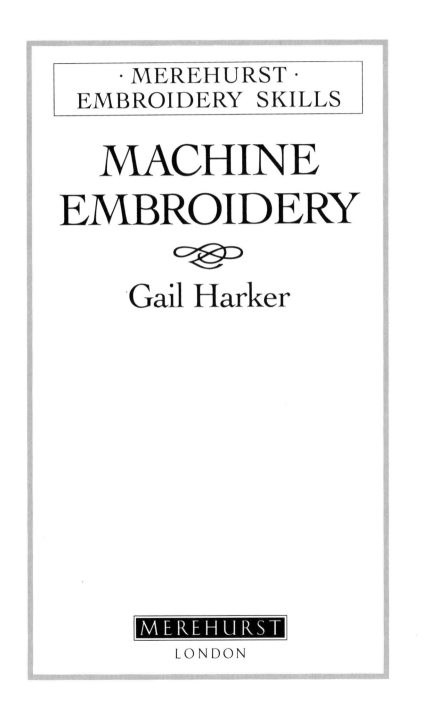

· MEREHURST ·
EMBROIDERY SKILLS

MACHINE EMBROIDERY

Gail Harker

MEREHURST

LONDON

This book is dedicated to my father, Steve Swabuk, whose writing has always inspired me to be creative. It is intended as a *starter book* for machine embroidery on the domestic sewing machine. Different machines accomplish the techniques shown here in different ways, so get to know your own machine – intimately. I have seen with many of my students that, although they may have excellent design ideas, they often have difficulty in transferring a concept to fabric. More often than not, this difficulty results from an inadequate knowledge of the basic machine embroidery vocabulary, as applied to their particular sewing machine.

The old saying, 'Rules were made to be broken', is certainly true of creative machine embroidery. But, before breaking the rules, know what the rules are!

Published 1990 by Merehurst Limited
Ferry House
51–57 Lacy Road
Putney
London SW15 1PR

© Copyright 1990 Merehurst Limited
ISBN 1 85391 057 0
Reprinted 1990

Edited by Diana Brinton
Designed by Bill Mason
Photography by Stewart Grant
(except pages 6/7)
Drawings by Lindsay Blow
Typesetting by Rowland Phototypesetting Limited,
Bury St Edmunds, Suffolk
Colour Separation by
Scantrans Pte Limited, Singapore
Printed in Italy by
New Interlitho SpA, Milan

CONTENTS

INTRODUCTION TO MACHINE EMBROIDERY

We've come a long way since 1755! It seems incredible that more than 200 years have passed since British Patent number 701 was granted to Charles F. Weisenthal, in 1755, for a machine to facilitate embroidery. This was the first sewing machine; so domestic sewing machine users owe the development of the sewing machine to embroidery.

Some years later, in 1790, Thomas Saint invented a machine that formed a chain stitch. This machine imitated tambour embroidery, a technique ordinarily worked by hand, with a tool called a tambour hook. Elias Howe's invention, in 1845, of a two-thread lockstitch machine resulted in a shift away from using chain stitch machines as general purpose sewing machines.

Thousands of sewing machine patents were issued, in many countries, and the sewing machine was one of the first products of the industrial age to cause strikes. A Frenchman, Thimonnier, in 1830, employed 80 machines stitching army clothing. These machines were destroyed in a tailors' uprising because the tailors feared that the automation would ruin their profession. Canada's first organized strike was fomented in 1852 as a result of the introduction of a sewing machine into a tailoring establishment.

Toward the end of the 19th century, machine embroidery stirred artistic excitement. This excitement came mostly as a result of the efforts of the Singer Sewing Machine Company, which used every opportunity to popularize and sell machines. The embroideries produced in Singer's workrooms were primarily intended to provide prestige and to advertise the capabilities of the Singer machine, but they popularized domestic machine embroidery.

In the 1930s, Dorothy Benson (a teacher in Singer's London workrooms) trained embroiderers and created work that was to have a lasting influence on machine embroidery. A particularly outstanding student of hers was Rebecca Crompton, some of whose machine-embroidered panels are displayed at the Victoria and Albert Museum

Dorothy Benson was to have a lasting influence on the embroidery world, both through her teaching and her work. (Photograph courtesy of the Dorking branch of the Embroiderers' Guild.)

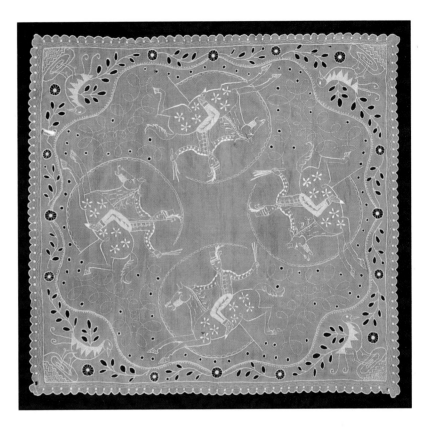

Through the work of Rebecca Crompton, machine embroidery achieved artistic credibility and began to be accepted by the established art colleges as an art form with great potential. (Photograph courtesy of the Dorking branch of the Embroiderers' Guild.)

in London. The impact of the introduction of machines powered by electric motors was now beginning to take effect, and the amount of hard labour involved in the production of machine embroidery was massively reduced.

The 20th-century invention of the swing-needle machine, was perhaps the most revolutionary and exciting development in the short history of the sewing machine. The swing-needle was a needle that could move from side to side and make a zigzag stitch or even a close satin stitch. Following the zigzag machines, came automatic, or programmed, patterns. Then came the electronic sewing machine, with all of the trappings of space-age sophistication, including computers, that could possibly be applied to sewing machines.

Where are we today?

With all of the gadgetry of the new, space-age machines and programmed designs, it is not unreasonable to ask: what is the excitement of machine embroidery all about, today? It is creativity! The scope offered to the free machine embroiderer of today is vast, especially when compared to the limited possibilities open to the technicians of the past. Today's machines are very precise instruments; the end result of intensive development over the past 200 years. Modern machines have benefited from new technology to such an extent that the technical skill required to operate modern machines is not nearly as great as that needed to get good results from vintage machines. This makes it possible for virtually anyone to learn to operate a modern machine and create work of outstanding beauty and interest.

Today's machine embroiderers have at their disposal an immense variety of materials never before seen in the embroidery world. A growing range of fabrics and threads is now available on the market. Many manufacturers are becoming more sensitive to machine embroiderers' needs.

In order to develop this medium, we should have a sense of fabric and the relationship of fabric to threads. We should experiment with the manipulation and reshaping of fabric through stitching. Textures can be created through the stitching of fine, delicate lines or circles, by crunchy, free satin stitch, or, indeed, by whatever stirs your artistic sense.

We should investigate the possibilities of making our own fabrics through weaving, felt making and other techniques. The addition of machine embroidery to a fabric of one's own creation can contribute a strength and integrity of design not otherwise available.

Usable and practical creations are well within the province of machine embroidery. Items can be made strong and durable as well as luxurious and delicate. It is important to expand our thinking and not be completely reliant on the age-old conventions of hand-embroidery techniques and materials. New techniques and space-age materials can assist us in exploiting this medium in revolutionary ways. We should be open to experimentation.

In Flying Over London, *by Lisa Whitlam, free running stitch is used very imaginatively and solidly to cover a large wall panel. Manipulation of the fabric becomes a feature.*

CHAPTER 1

AUTOMATIC AND FREE MACHINE EMBROIDERY

Throughout this book, reference will be made to two terms – automatic machine embroidery and free machine embroidery. In the first case, the feed dogs that feed the fabric under the needle are left up, and functional; in the case of free machining, they are lowered, so that they become inoperative.

The feed dogs can be shifted up or down mechanically on most machines, but if this is not possible on your model, a cover must be placed over the feed dogs so that they do not engage the fabric. Some manufacturers supply these covers, but if they are not available, the same effect may be achieved by covering the feed dogs with a piece of thin cardboard, taped down around the edges, or simply by applying transparent tape over them. (Remember to make a hole for the passage of the needle.)

Feed dogs must be up for automatic machining as for general sewing.

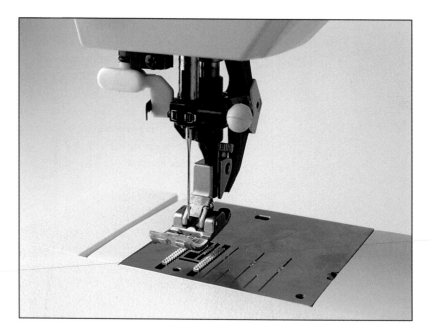

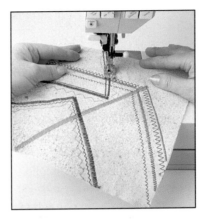

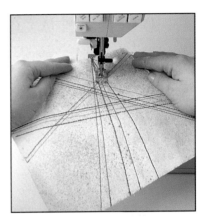

Automatic machining, using a zigzag sequence, with the presser foot attached.

Automatic machining, using the straight stitch sequence, with presser foot attached.

Automatic stitching

The numerous automatic stitches, both utility and decorative, that have been available on sewing machines for many years, can be used for creative machine embroidery. It is possible, however, to vary the application of these automatic stitches to create some very individual pieces of work. Automatic patterns may be shortened or lengthened, made wider or more narrow, depending upon the creative imagination of the embroiderer. In the case of computerized machines that allow individual pattern programming, it is possible to program unique stitches or stitch sequences.

Free machining

Free machining is generally covered in manufacturers' manuals under darning. It normally involves only two stitches – running stitch and zigzag – worked with the feed dogs down and the fabric, which is usually held in a frame, moved under the needle by hand. The combination of frame movement and foot pedal pressure allows you to vary the length of stitch and speed of sewing.

Know your machine

If you are consistently having problems with your machine, have it serviced. Explain to the service person that you are using the machine for embroidery; describe the types of threads being used and the effects that you are trying to obtain, and make it clear that you will need to adjust top and bobbin tensions. If the machine has any particular limitations, the service person will so advise you.

Above all, get to know your machine: no machine will do everything; not even a new one. Your own familiarity with your machine will dictate what is, and what is not, possible.

Anyone in the market for a new sewing machine will find that there is a vast number of machines, with manufacturers offering competing claims regarding new capabilities and advances in technology. It would be rather more easy to make a reasoned choice if the terms used by all manufacturers had the same meaning, but unfortunately they do not. What follows is not an exhaustive study of all the machines in the marketplace, but it covers some of the most common terms and capabilities, with the aim of making it a bit easier to understand what is available.

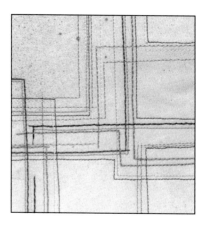

Straight stitch machines will only make a straight, general purpose sewing stitch.

Straight stitch machines

These are basic machines that will only make a straight sewing stitch.

Zigzag machines

Zigzag machines have a needle bar that moves from side to side as you sew. These machines will do both straight stitch and zigzag.

Semi-automatic machines

These machines will do a basic zigzag stitch, plus other utility stitches. The utility stitches are, generally, accomplished through the use of shaped discs called cams. These may be either built-in or changeable by the user. The shapes on the cam control the side to side movement of the needle bar, varying the stitch width and producing patterns.

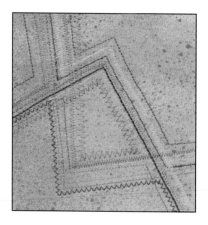

Zigzag machines will make both straight and zigzag stitches.

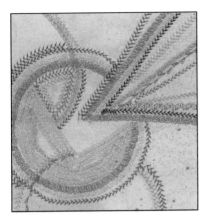

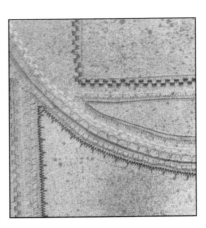

Semi-automatic machines will allow stitch width variations while sewing.

Fully automatic machines will automatically control the feed dogs for forward and reverse feed of the fabric, combining this facility with a controlled side-to-side motion of the needle bar. These facilities allow automatic pattern generation. Fully electronic machines will produce all of the stitches of the automatic machines, but in addition to this they are able to vary both stitch width and length while sewing.

Computerized machines are fully electronic and conform to those capabilities. Some machines allow the user to program individual designs and patterns by creating original instructions to the feed dogs and needle bar.

Fully automatic machines

The fully automatic machines will do straight stitching and zigzag, as well as having the facility to produce a wide variety of decorative stitches.

Electronic machines

The use of the term electronic has developed into an advertising buzz word: it can be used in any number of contexts because it conjures up concepts of technological advancement. Some manufacturers will claim their machine is electronic if any electronic control circuit is used in the machine, but electronic control circuits are used in a number of applications from manufacturer to manufacturer.

13

In the older electric machines, the sewing speed is controlled by varying the amount of electricity, or power, to the motor. Slow speeds entailed lower power and a loss of needle penetration. Electronic speed control allows full power to the motor, regardless of speed, resulting in full needle penetration power at slower sewing speeds.

Fully electronic machines not only have electronic speed control, but, as far as most manufacturers are concerned, they also have electronic control circuits, operated by push button, for the needle bar and feed dogs. In other words, the sewing speed, the rate at which the fabric feeds through, and the needle bar operation are all electronically coordinated.

Computerized machines

Computerized machines are at the leading edge of sewing machine technology and are the most expensive models available. A wide variety of patterns are pre-programmed into micro-chip control circuits which, for the most part, replace the cams used in automatic machines, controlling feed, needle swing and speed. Some machines have a memory that stores and recalls stitches and patterns, so they can be programmed to create individual patterns and store them in the memory for later use. Some machines will have replaceable, plug-in, pattern modules, available as an option at extra cost.

Buyer's checklist

Free machine embroidery may be done on almost any sewing machine, but the following are points to consider before you buy a new machine.

- Check whether the feed dogs can be lowered into the needle plate or not.

- If the feed dogs cannot be lowered, ensure that there is a cover plate that can be used to cover the feed dogs. Check for protrusions that might catch or snag the embroidery frame.

- For machine embroidery, a flat bed is preferred. If the bed is sloping, ensure that the embroidery frame can be held tightly to the bed of the machine, with no gaps.

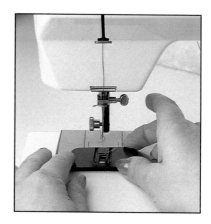

Cover plate/darning plate: different names may be given to this plate, which is normally supplied as an accessory with the machine. The plate is used to cover the feed dogs when darning or ~ in the case of models that do not allow the feed dogs to be lowered ~ during free machining. The plate may be attached by clips or a screw.

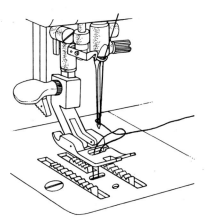

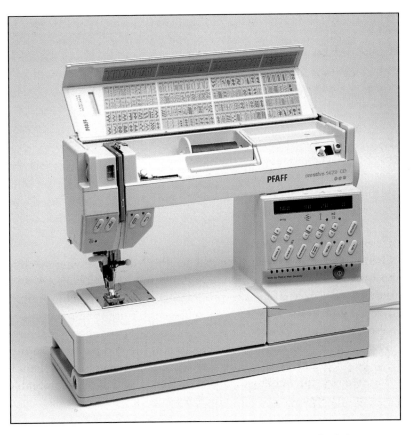

It is advisable to be completely familiar with the names of all of the parts on your machine. Using the manual for your own machine, identify each part, so that no confusion exists for any of the instructions that will follow.

The presser foot applies pressure to the fabric so that the feed dogs engage the fabric, feeding it at the correct rate as the machine makes automatic stitches. (Some machines have a pressure control, to vary the pressure applied to the presser foot.) The presser foot should be raised for threading the top of the machine. When free machining with the presser foot removed, the presser bar *must* be in the lowered, or down, position.

The feed dogs move back and forth in a cylindrical, up and down motion, feeding the fabric under the needle during conventional or automatic stitching. They are lowered or covered for free machining.

Needle plate/throat plate: different manufacturers have their own names for this plate, which has slots through which the feed dogs and needle operate.

- Ensure that the bobbin tension can be varied. Some bobbin cases may be removed from the machine and adjusted by turning the set screw on the side of the bobbin case. Other cases are fixed in the machine where the bobbin is fitted. Some of these are adjusted with a set screw with a graduated tension scale, while other machines have a tension screw but no numerical scale. Since bobbins are changed and tension varied with great regularity, it also pays to make sure that the bobbin is easily accessible.

Automatic stitching

Before beginning to embroider, always set your machine up for a test, adjusting it to produce *perfect straight stitch*. Experienced machine embroiderers have all learned the importance of stitching small trial pieces as a check on machine operations and techniques.

Threading With the presser bar up, to open the top tension discs, thread the top thread (needle thread) through the guides, according to the manual for your machine. Load the bobbin with thread, of the same size and of a contrasting colour to the top thread, and put it in the machine. Ensure that the needle is straight and sharp. Bring the top and bobbin threads to the sewing surface and place the fabric under the needle.

Machine controls Lower the presser bar; check that the feed dogs are up; set the tension to normal (between 3 and 5), and set the stitch control for straight stitch.

Machining Sew a line of straight stitch. If the top thread shows through the bottom of the fabric, gradually increase the top tension and sew another row of stitching until no top thread is visible on the bottom. If the bobbin thread appears on the top of the fabric, gradually increase bobbin tension until the bobbin thread is no longer visible on the top.

Top and bottom tension for normal sewing

It is essential to be able to adjust tensions on your machine, although some manuals may advise against this. Some machines have what is termed universal tension, and in theory such machines do not require adjustment, but in practice it is vital to be able to adjust tensions for specific machine embroidery techniques.

Top (upper) tension

Top tension may be adjusted through the use of a numbered dial or knob. The scale usually ranges from 0 to 10: 0 represents no top tension; 3 to 5 normal tension, and 6 to 10 very tight or high tension. Some machines have no numerical scale at all, having instead a

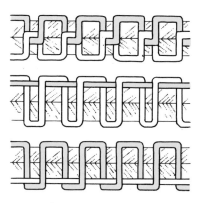

When no contrasting thread appears on the top or bottom of the fabric, the perfect straight stitch has been accomplished. Some machines may not make a perfect straight stitch: if you encounter problems, refer to the section on Troubleshooting (page 124).

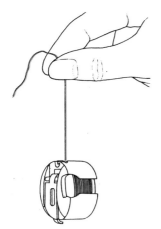

The bobbin thread should not spool out through the weight of the bobbin case alone. If the thread spools rapidly, the bobbin tension is too loose. If the thread does not spool out, the tension is too tight.

simple '+' or '−' indication on either side of a central or normal setting.

Bobbin tension for removable bobbin cases

Wind the bobbin with the required thread and insert it into the bobbin case.

Most bobbin cases have a set screw and a tension screw. The set screw holds the tension band in place. The tension screw is the one that may need adjustment. When adjusting the tension screw, only turn the screw a half turn for each adjustment. Holding the bobbin case with the open side (the side where the bobbin is inserted) facing your body, turn the tension screw – clockwise to increase tension or anti-clockwise to reduce tension. Take care: this tiny screw has a tendency to pop out and is easily lost.

Some machines have a built-in, non-removable bobbin case, which lies flat in the machine, under the needle plate. There will generally be a tension screw alongside a numbered scale. To adjust the tension, use the machine screwdriver: '0' indicates little or no tension and higher numbers indicate increasing tensions (other machines use a '+' or '−' system).

Fabrics for machine embroidery

A medium- to heavy-weight cotton fabric is ideal for first attempts at machine embroidery. Polycotton is not generally recommended for machine embroidery, due to its lightness and tendency to pucker.

After your first efforts, once you are beginning to feel at ease with the technique, it is useful to experiment with as many types of fabric as possible. This will encourage creative ideas about the applications of various fabrics. Try cottons of all weights, silks, satins, acetate, linen, net, 100 per cent nylon, curtaining, rayon, plastic sheeting, paper, net bags from the grocer, scrims of all weights, butter and cheese muslin, leather, vinyl, lace, ribbons, velvets and interfacings. In other words, anything through which the needle will pass is suitable for machine embroidery.

You will find that every fabric has its own particular properties, and slight machine adjustments may be required for each of them.

Some fabrics will require backing in order to provide the stiffness necessary to support satin stitch or heavy automatic embroidery. For this purpose, iron-on or paper interfacing may be used.

Where very stretchy fabric is used, it may be advisable to tack it to a firm, medium-weight, cotton backing, before framing and stitching. Fabrics with a lot of stretch will be very difficult to frame evenly, and when the fabric is removed from the frame and the tension is released, the stitching may disappear into the fabric. You will find that some fabrics are too thin to be used on their own for machine embroidery. In these cases, the fabric may be doubled to provide support for the embroidery.

If the thread shows a tendency to drag through a particular fabric or paper, it may help if you change to a needle of a larger size.

Take note of the effect of using heavy threads on light fabrics: very fine fabric, unless mounted on a backing, will pucker if a very heavy thread is used to cover the whole piece. If the weight of the thread is matched to that of the fabric, a more even and consistent stitch will be produced. It is useful, at this stage in the development of your machine embroidery repertoire, to begin a reference book. A loose-leaf binder can be used to collect samples of fabrics, threads, techniques, tensions and machine settings.

Embroidery materials may include silk, silk cotton, mercerized cotton, cotton muslin, cotton organdie, nylon organza, pelmet vilene, acetate satin, light-weight wool, cotton velvet, silk taffeta, leather, nylon net, felt, heavy-weight cotton, ribbons and machine embroidery threads.

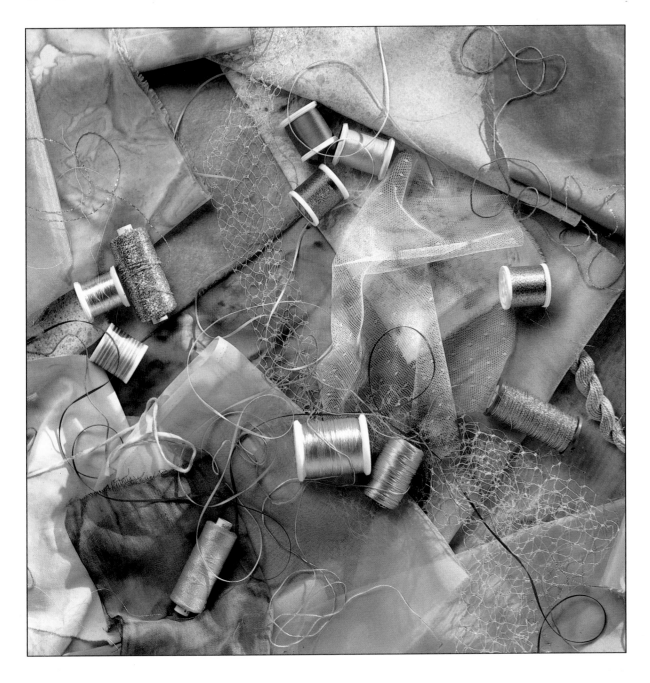

Interfacings

It happens so often: someone watches a sewing machine demonstration; sees wonderful stitches being created; purchases the machine and takes it home, only to find that the stitch patterns are not quite up to the quality of the demonstration. What that person has probably failed to observe is that the stitch demonstration was worked on very stiff fabric or on several layers of fabric.

Often, automatic decorative stitching will be very heavy and can pucker the fabric upon which it is produced. One must therefore ensure that sufficient stiffening or backing is present to offset this tendency. Fortunately, there are products that can assist machine embroiderers with these problems. A number of manufacturers produce paper interfacings variously known as Stitch-and-Tear or by other trade names.

Satin stitch and many of the intricate computerized patterns available on a wide range of machines require backing of this type. If these products are not readily available, ordinary paper may be used, but it will not tear away so neatly.

Other products that may be used are the iron-on, or fused, interlinings. These, however, will alter the feel and pliability of the fabric to which they are applied.

Experiment with all the options. Fusible interfacings are available in light, medium and heavy weights: your local fabric shop should be able to offer you a good selection.

Pelmet interfacing is a very thick, stiff product, intended to give pelmets more rigidity. Because of this stiffness, it can be used without a frame for both automatic and free embroidery techniques. Creative stitching can be done on this fabric.

Double-sided fusible interfacing is ideal for bonding appliqué shapes to a background fabric. This obviates the need to baste appliqué pieces to the background.

Vanishing muslin

This is a stiffened, chemically treated material that disappears when it is heated with an iron. Because of this property, stitches may be applied to the material which, when ironed, will leave behind only

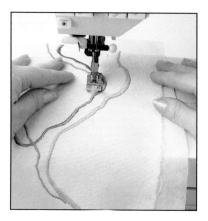

1 To use paper interfacing, or simple typing paper, to strengthen the fabric during stitching, place an appropriately-sized piece of interfacing under the fabric to be embroidered, between the fabric and the needle plate. Stitch the pattern or design on the fabric.

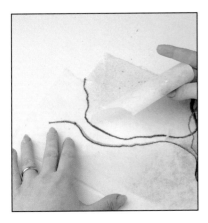

2 Turn the fabric to the reverse side and carefully tear away the interfacing. The product will neatly separate from the work, leaving a consistent pattern without puckers.

If you choose, you can use an interfacing as the background fabric on which to embroider. Most interfacings are very receptive to dyes. In this panel by June Lovesy, interfacing has been dyed, torn into strips, and reassembled as a background fabric. The top lace panel is worked on hot-water-soluble fabric.

the stitches that have been applied. As an aid in designing, patterns may be drawn on the fabric. This material may be used to stiffen or support other fabric while doing machine embroidery. Instead of using a hot iron, you can dissolve the muslin by placing it in an oven heated to 150°C (300°F). When the muslin turns brown, it may be gently brushed away with a soft toothbrush.

21

Threads for machine embroidery

Machine embroidery threads are quite different from ordinary sewing threads. Threads manufactured exclusively for machine embroidery do not normally have the high twist required of ordinary threads. Because they do not have this high twist, they lack tensile strength, are softer, and have a tendency to spread and cover areas with fewer passes of the needle.

The numbering system used for machine embroidery threads is the same as that used for dressmakers' threads, being based on weight, but because of the looser twist, the end result is very different. A No. 40 dressmakers' thread, for instance, is much too heavy for machine embroidery and would tangle and clog hopelessly as stitches piled up. A No. 40 machine embroidery thread, by comparison, would pass through the machine with ease and would cause no problems. A No. 50 dressmakers' thread could be used for machine embroidery as this is a medium-weight thread, finer than No. 40 dressmakers' thread, and would pass through the machine. A No. 50 machine embroidery thread would, however, appear much finer than the No. 50 dressmakers', and is in fact the finest grade that is readily available. When machine embroidery threads are not readily available, it is possible to use dressmakers' threads.

The properties of the two types of threads have been developed for their very specific purposes. Machine embroidery threads – except for the heavier weights – lack strength, so it would not be advisable to use them for ordinary sewing. On the other hand, the soft, pliable nature of those very threads provides a nice, even, lustrous coverage when used in embroidery.

Machine embroidery threads are produced in a wide variety of fibres. These range from 100 per cent cotton, viscose rayon with a high tensile strength, nylon, polyamide and silk, to wool and wool-and-acrylic mixes, as well as metallic threads. This allows you to select a thread with a mat, sheen or metallic finish – whichever is right for the design and the end use.

When it is desirable to use heavier threads, they should be wound onto the bobbin. Six-stranded hand-embroidery cottons, floss or silk may be used in this way, as may perlé threads (all weights),

Special machine embroidery threads may be used on the top of the machine (above), but other threads may also be used for special effects. This includes heavier threads, such as tatting, perlé or crochet cotton (right).

and some knitting and crochet yarns, as well as heavier metal threads, provided that the latter are not so wiry that they will not feed properly.

Some heavier threads, such as tatting cotton, buttonhole twist and heavier machine embroidery threads, may be used on the top of the machine, providing a larger-sized needle or a needle with an enlarged eye (a topstitching needle) is used.

Bobbin thread

Regardless of the type of thread used on the top, and unless special effects are required, use machine embroidery cotton Nos 30 or 50 in the bobbin. Since this thread is not seen, it does not matter what colour is used. If the back of the work is to be seen, use the same thread in the bobbin as on the top. Any type of machine embroidery is finer and easier to work with machine embroidery cotton in the bobbin.

Hints on thread usage

Top thread breakage This usually occurs because machines are set up for general sewing with high-strength sewing threads and the top tension is too high/tight for machine embroidery.

Try reducing top tension by degrees. You might start at tension 3, but it could be necessary to reduce to 1. Each machine is different, but remember that adjusting the tensions does not harm the machine.

Needles Some of the specialized threads will require the use of larger needles, but for normal embroidery try a size 90 (14 US/Eng.). It is good practice to change needles often when using metallic threads. Ensure that needles are not bent nor 'burred', in other words with nicks or sharp edges. You can find these by running a finger down the needle. Be sure, when inserting needles, that they are seated as high in the needle slot as they will go and orientated in the proper direction.

Uncontrolled thread spool-off Some of the metallic and rayon threads have a tendency to spool off the reel in an uncontrolled fashion. Some machine manufacturers have dealt with this problem by adding an extra thread guide. This is often designed to clip on the reel holder. If this is not available, the problem may be solved by taping a tapestry needle alongside the reel, or behind it and set slightly higher than the reel. Alternatively, a piece of felt, cut to fit under the reel, will sometimes help the problem. Some of the newer machines have horizontally mounted reel holders. These can often solve spool-off problems and are helpful to machine embroiderers.

Threads shred on the last guide If this is a problem, do not use this guide, which leads to the needle, if at all possible.

The addition of an extra thread guide is a useful aid if threads have a tendency to unreel in an uncontrolled fashion.

Machine embroidery needles

It is important to the machine embroiderer to have a good under-standing of the full range of sewing machine needles, which includes several designed for special applications.

Continental and US/English needle sizes

Continental	60	65	70	75	80	90	100	110	120
US/English	8	9	10	11	12	14	16	18	20
	Very Fine				**Medium**				**Very Heavy**

The needle size is normally selected according to the weight and type of fabric being used. Size 90 (14) is the middle of the range and is used for sewing fabrics of medium weight. A medium size is a good choice for machine embroidery beginners, because it is more resistant to flexing and bending during free machine embroidery than a finer needle. Fine needles have a tendency to bend, break, miss stitches and shred machine embroidery threads. One of the most common causes of skipped stitches is that the needle has been inserted backwards or not high enough, so take care to insert needles correctly. It is important to change needles frequently when sewing on synthetic fabrics or using metallic threads.

While the general charts matching needle sizes to fabrics are useful for dressmakers, they do not normally apply to machine embroidery. The machine embroiderer must select a needle that will allow the use of modern machine embroidery threads. These may incorporate fibre blends and twisted metallic threads and, as a result, a heavier needle may be required to accommodate them. Even though you may use a 90 (14) needle initially, it may be advisable to increase the size or use a topstitch needle if you encounter problems with threads.

In addition to US/English and Continental sizes, needle selection is further confused through the use of different sewing systems. Thankfully, only one system is used on most modern zigzag machines. This is designated on needle packaging as 130/705H. Caution must be exercised, however: check your own machine manual for the correct needle system identification. The following lists a selection of special needles, with some of their embroidery applications.

Twin needles These are produced in various sizes and with the needles spaced varying distances apart. In addition to the system number, the spacing and needle size will be noted on the packaging. For example, the notation, 1.6/80 indicates size 80 needles, spaced 1.6mm apart. To thread twin needles, two threads are routed through the top of the machine in the same way as for single needle sewing. The two threads are then threaded through separate sides of the tension discs and each is taken through one needle. The bobbin contains one thread. The effect of the twin needle is to create two parallel rows of stitches, and it may be used to create some decorative and zigzag stitches.

Take care to check, manually, that the needle will pass through the needle plate, before making automatic zigzag stitches. Some machines may have special threading instructions for twin needle operations, so read your manual.

Triple needles Not all sewing machines will accommodate triple needles, so be sure to refer to your own sewing machine manual. The effect of the triple needle is to create three parallel lines of stitches, with three threads through the top of the machine. These needles may be used for decorative and zigzag stitches.

Twin needles may be used to produce unusual and creative machine embroidery effects. The distance between the shafts varies, as does the size of the needles. Triple needles may not be usable on all machines, so check your manual. Many fine effects are possible with these special needles.

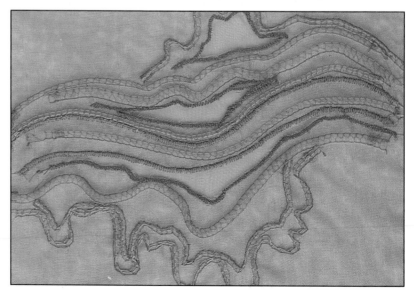

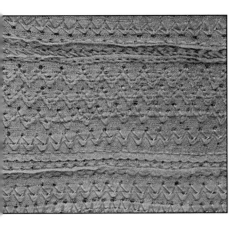

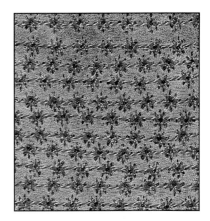

Double wing needles (left) are normally used in hemstitching, but, again, the experimenting machine embroiderer will be able to produce exciting patterns.

Single wing needles (right) perforate fabrics such as lawn, organdie and muslin, creating interesting decorative effects.

Ballpoint needle Synthetic fabrics and knits can resist 'sharp' needle penetration and cause skipped stitches. Ballpoint needles were developed to overcome this problem: the ballpoint pushes the fibres aside rather than piercing and splitting them. Always be sure to buy the correct type for your machine.

Jeans needle This needle, with its sharp and tapered point, was designed to pierce dense fabrics, such as denim. It is a very useful needle for embroidery on heavy fabrics.

Leather needle The leather needle has a wedge-shaped cutting edge which helps it to pierce tough materials like leather, oil cloth, vinyl and other plastic materials.

Topstitch needle This is a special design with a larger eye than a needle of its size would normally have. The needle is used for automatic and free machining and is ideal for accommodating heavier threads.

Single wing The 'wing' refers to a flattening and widening of the needle shaft, which enables this needle to make an enlarged entry hole and decoratively perforate the fabric as it sews fine fabrics, such as lawn and organdie. This is a very good needle for free machining.

Double wing The double wing needle is similar to a twin needle, except that one of the needles is shaped like a single wing needle.

Feet and attachments

The feet and attachments named here are particularly applicable to automatic, decorative and free machine embroidery.

Satin stitch foot The satin stitch presser foot is designed with a shallow groove on the underside of the foot to allow clearance of the high pile created by the stitches. This allows the fabric to feed through evenly.

Darning foot Although most machines will allow free machining without the use of a foot, the idiosyncrasies of individual machines may demand the use of the darning foot for free machining. The darning foot assists in stabilizing fabric and also acts as a safety guard to keep fingers from passing under the needle.

Tailor tacking foot This foot is also used for making fringes in the automatic stitching mode. It has a high ridge in the centre, which creates a high looped fringe when satin stitch is applied.

Teflon foot/roller foot Either of these may be used for automatic stitching on such fabrics as vinyl, plastics or leather.

Open toe foot This foot is sometimes called an embroidery foot or appliqué foot. The toe of the foot is shorter than other feet to allow the embroiderer to see the production of the stitch.

Pin tuck foot Used in automatic stitching, this foot has from one to seven grooves on the underside to facilitate sewing raised seams with a twin needle. The grooves engage previously sewn line(s), while the needles sew further, parallel lines.

Eyelet plate Usually attached to the sewing plate, this has a small cylindrical protrusion that is placed through a small hole pierced through the fabric. Zigzag stitch is sewn around the edges until an even satin stitch is achieved. This plate is used only on swing needle machines.

Fringe and rug making fork The fork is used to produce a fringe in the automatic stitching mode. This fringe may be left as it is or clipped to produce an unlooped fringe.

Some of the more useful feet and attachments used for machine embroidery, clockwise from the top left: darning foot, eyelet plate, tailor tacking foot, regular sewing foot, pin tuck foot, open appliqué foot, teflon foot.

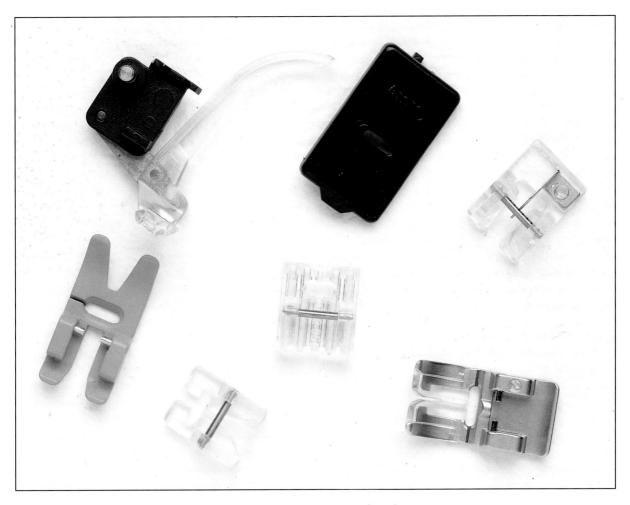

Circular sewing attachment In the automatic stitching mode, this attachment is used to produce precise circular patterns. Fabric used with this attachment must be placed in an embroidery frame. A pin is inserted through the fabric to a locating hole some distance from the needle. Any automatic stitch may then be sewn, while the work rotates about the pin, creating a circular pattern.

Walking foot Sometimes called an even feed attachment, this feeds layers of bulky or slippery fabric through evenly.

Machine embroidery frames

Unless the fabric is very stiff, it is essential to use a frame to secure it for free machining. A frame will hold fabric tightly to control the material any time the feed dogs are lowered or disengaged and the presser foot is removed. Frames are also an aid in manipulating fabric during free machine embroidery.

As a general rule, the smaller the frame, the more tightly the fabric may be mounted, but whatever the size of the frame, you must allow an adequate overlap around the sides.

Round frames

Round embroidery frames or hoops come in a variety of sizes and materials. They may be made of wood, plastic or metal. Wood and metal frames generally have a knurled screw on the outer ring to adjust the frame for varying fabric thickness and tightness. Some wooden types are too deep to pass under the needle with ease. If this is the case, cut a notch in the edge to allow the needle to pass into the centre of the frame. It is advisable to bind the inner ring of wood frames with narrow bias tape, stitched at the end to secure it. The tape binding helps to reduce slippage of the framed fabric.

Plastic frames are made with a groove on the inner face of the ring, which receives a metal, sprung, inner ring. These frames are recom-

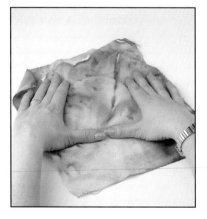

1 Place the outer ring on a firm, flat surface and lay fabric over this ring.

2 Press the inner ring into the outer ring. Ensure that the fabric is stretched taut by gently pulling and stretching it around the ring. It may be necessary to tighten the tension screw on the frame. Press the inner ring slightly below the outer ring so that the fabric makes close contact with the needle plate.

mended for finer fabrics, such as fine cotton and silks. However, the largest size that will adequately secure the fabric for free machining is about 12cm. Ensure that the frame allows the fabric to lie directly on the needle plate, with no gaps.

Free machining without a frame

Very stiff fabrics may sometimes be free machined without a frame. Fabrics generally suitable for stitching without frames include canvas, pelmet interfacing, buckram or lighter fabric that has been stiffened with roller blind spray. For safety's sake, it may be advisable to use the darning foot to protect your fingers.

Other equipment

Scissors Use dressmakers' for fabric cutting and small sharp scissors for appliqué and other intricate cutting requirements.

Tweezers Useful for removing threads that may be wound around the bobbin case or jammed in the feed dogs.

Lint brush These are usually supplied with the machine to remove the lint that builds up around the bobbin case and feed dogs.

Sewing machine oil Some newer machines are self-lubricating. Others require oil. Use oil sparingly and use only sewing machine oil.

Bobbin case It is very convenient to have an extra bobbin case. Retain one case at normal tension, the other at much looser tension for special effects.

Bobbins It is very convenient to have several bobbins wound with thread for rapid exchange.

Spray glue Very light applications of spray glue are useful to hold fabrics together for stitching and help to hold appliqué shapes in place as you sew.

Embroidery frames and other useful equipment for machine embroidery: frames, scissors, tweezers, lint brush, sewing machine oil, extra bobbin case, bobbins, pins, fabric marking pencils, stitch ripper and pins.

CHAPTER 2

AUTOMATIC STITCHING

Quilting by machine

Some traditionalists believe that to quilt by machine is, somehow, cheating. Perhaps they will cling to their opinion, but machine quilters have created some truly outstanding works – no apologies to anyone. Machine quilting removes much of the laborious work and time required for handstitching, and there are many ways in which the machine embroiderer might undertake quilting. The range of machine embroidery techniques may, for example, be used in combination on quilted works, so once you have familiarized yourself with basic techniques, try experimenting with others.

Fabrics
Fabrics made from natural fibres are generally preferable for quilting. Man-made fibres are usually too springy for successful quilting.

The top fabric should be closely-woven fabric of a plain colour. It can be cotton, silk, satin, fine leather, suede, linen, fine wool, a wool/cotton mixture or some types of knitted fabric.

The middle layer can be of polyester, cotton or silk batting.

The bottom fabric may be the same fabric as the top layer or a fabric of similar weight.

Threads
Use silk threads or good quality polyester No. 50 on silk fabric. For quilting on cotton, use dressmakers' cotton No. 50 on top and in the bobbin, or transparent nylon on top with polyester in the bobbin.

It is not advisable to use machine embroidery threads for quilting unless the piece is intended for decorative purposes only. If the piece is designed for regular use, dressmakers' threads will prove stronger and more lasting.

To make Bobbi in the Rain, *I first enlarged and simplified a photograph of my daughter. A pleasing pattern was developed by moving paper cut-outs around. The little girl shapes were cut from dyed fabric and appliquéd on the background fabric. The quilting lines represent rain, and were stitched in a variety of straight and zigzag patterns.*

Needles Ensure that the thread can pass freely through the eye of the needle without shredding and that the point does not make too large a hole in the fabric – try a size 80(12) or 90(14).

Stitches You can use straight stitch, zigzag stitch, or any decorative utility stitch, provided this allows the fabric to move freely under the needle without causing it to buckle or pucker during stitching.

Foot Use the presser foot for general sewing.

Tensions Reduce the top tension slightly and set the bobbin tension at normal.

Stitch length If a straight stitch is used, the stitch should be lengthened. On most machines, a stitch length setting of 3 (approximately 3mm) will provide a sufficiently long stitch. This is to accommodate the extra thickness of the batting. Thicker batting will demand longer stitches. Closely-spaced satin stitches may prove difficult through layered fabric, but a backing of paper interfacing will help.

Preparation

Baste the top, middle and back layers together, working in a grid or in the form of a cross and always stitching from the centre to the edges. Very thorough basting is required. The chosen design may be transferred either before or after basting.

Machining

On large quilts, the piece should be rolled from each end to the centre, so that one half of the piece can be sewn from the centre to the outside edge, scrolling from one roll to the other. When the outside edge is reached, re-roll and work to the other outside edge. The piece may be machined in one direction at a time, with the unsewn roll gradually being opened out as sewing progresses, much as ancient manuscript scrolls were read. When all of the machining in one direction, for example lengthways, has been done, the roll should be unrolled and re-rolled so that it can then be stitched crossways.

Smaller pieces or squares will not need to be rolled and will also allow free designs to be applied, because the work can be manipulated during stitching.

This quilt by Annwyn Dean features shadow quilting, made with straight stitch and satin stitch.

Satin stitch

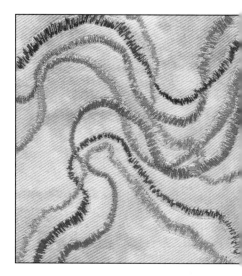

One of the most frequently ignored stitches on the machine seems to be the satin stitch. Satin stitch may be used for decorative purposes, edgings, appliqué or quilting. The following are some ideas for working successfully with satin stitch.

Satin stitch is a variation of the zigzag stitch. The width of the stitch is set on the stitch width control, but the stitch length control must be set for closely spaced stitches, to achieve full coverage without spaces between stitches. Some machines allow width and length variations while sewing. This facility permits a varying width of the satin stitch line. The sheen of the closely spaced threads creates a lustrous effect.

Fabrics Any fabric may be used for satin stitch, but unless it is a heavy fabric, such as heavy cotton or denim, it will pucker under the stresses of stitching. Steps must therefore be taken to reduce those stresses on lighter fabrics: depending upon the weight of the fabric, place under it either one or two layers of paper interfacing, of the type that can easily be torn away, then remove it after stitching; or stiffen the fabric with iron-on interfacing. The latter will, however, alter the feel of the fabric.

Threads Fine, soft embroidery threads, both on the top of the machine and in the bobbin, make the nicest satin stitches. Heavy threads can look clumsy and will have a tendency to clog the machine through stitch build-up.

Needle The needle size is dependent on the weight of fabric and the thread being used. Begin with a size 80(12) needle and experiment: the thread should not shred and the fabric should not cause the needle to flex back and forth. If these problems occur, change to a larger size of needle. A topstitching needle, with its elongated eye, can be used to combat thread shredding.

Foot Use the zigzag (satin stitch) presser foot.

Tensions Decrease the top tension so that only the top thread shows on the fabric.

In this photograph, taken to show the effects of loose bobbin tension, silver thread has been used and the bobbin tension has been loosened. The top – blue and pink thread – brings up the silver thread to produce a variegated effect. The top tension can also be tightened to produce the same effect.

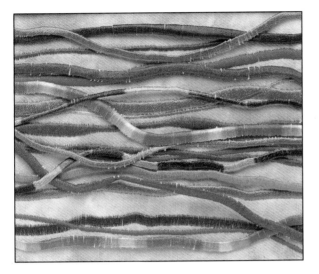

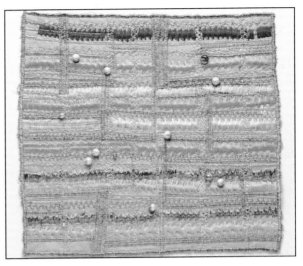

Satin stitch can be worked over typing or tracing paper or paper interfacing. The paper is torn away from either side of the very close satin stitch. If your satin stitch is not sufficiently close, go over the lines a second time.

Rows of satin stitch have here been worked by pivoting the fabric rapidly from side to side in an arc while the machine is operating, in this way distorting the stitch.

Stitch width Whatever you wish.

Stitch length This should be close enough for the stitches to lie side by side without gaps. If stitches pile up on each other and the fabric does not feed properly, extend the stitch length slightly.

Satin stitch variations

The satin stitch instructions just given are for traditional applications, but if you experiment with top and bobbin tensions, with different weights of threads and fabrics, and with stitch widths and lengths, you will discover your own original satin stitch variations. Even though the machine produces a straight line of satin stitch, the fabric does not have to follow that straight line, as you can manipulate it while the satin stitch is being formed.

Satin stitch edging for shapes

Satin stitch may be used to finish edges of fabric, either to prevent fraying or to provide a decorative edge. The machine is set up as for satin stitch, with certain exceptions, given below.

Fabric Almost any fabric may be used, though it is best to use a reasonably firm fabric for practising if you are a beginner. If the fabric is very light in weight, it may be advisable to double it and use featherweight non-woven interfacing or vanishing muslin.

Needle Start with the smallest needle that will allow the thread to pass without shredding: try 65(9) or 70(10) to start with. Large needles

Satin stitch edging

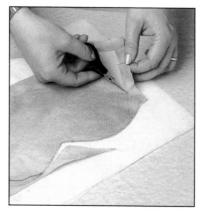

1 Using a pencil, transfer your pattern outline to the fabric. Attach two layers of paper interfacing to the back of your fabric. These may be either lightly sprayed with glue or hand basted. Sew a straight stitch, with a stitch length of approximately 1.5mm (¹⁄₁₆in.), along the pattern line marked on the fabric.

2 If it is desirable to be able to bend the shape into a particular form, a wire may be laid inside the line of straight stitch. Make a narrow zigzag stitch over the wire, then cut away the excess fabric from the shape, closely following the line of stitching. Do not cut away the paper interfacing.

3 Sew a close satin stitch along the inside edge of the shape. Ensure that the satin stitch covers the straight and zigzag stitches. If your machine will not produce a close satin stitch, increase the stitch length slightly and sew around the shape a second time.

have a tendency to perforate and weaken the fabric along the stitching line.

Tensions It is desirable for the stitches to lock along one side of the row on the underside. To achieve this, the tensions must be adjusted so that the top thread is pulled to the underside and therefore covers both sides of the fabric. Gradually reduce the top tension until it is possible to see the locked stitch on the underside of the fabric along one edge of the stitching. If this effect cannot be achieved through reduction of the top tension alone, the bobbin tension may need to be increased. Some machines may lock the satin stitch down the centre of the stitching at the back, rather than along one edge. In this case, use threads of the same colour on the top and in the bobbin.

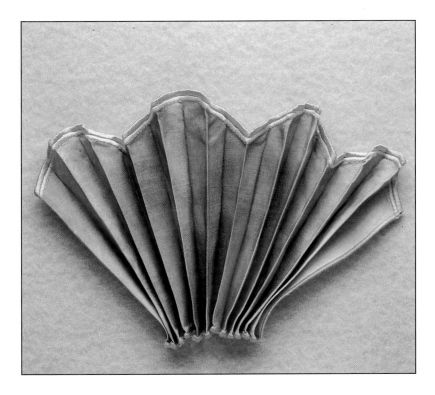

4 Gently tear the interfacing from the back of your shape. This will leave the three-dimensional shape. The success of this technique lies in the closeness of the satin stitch, which conceals the fibres of the interfacing.

Raised satin stitch – loops and fringe

This technique employs the tailor tacking foot, sometimes called a fringe foot. This foot was originally designed to enable dressmakers to make basting stitches. Embroiderers can use this foot in a much more creative way by sewing a satin stitch over it to produce loops and fringing. Experiments with tensions and threads will create some very individual effects and textures, and these can be combined with other techniques. Start by setting your machine up as for satin stitch.

Fabric Use a heavy-weight fabric or add a backing.

Threads Any type of machine embroidery thread may be used. Stiff or metallic threads will produce a loop or fringe that stands erect. Machine embroidery cotton is recommended for the bobbin.

Foot Use a tailor tacking foot.

Stitch width Narrow satin stitch will produce a full fringe or loop; a wide satin stitch will produce a more widely-spaced fringe or loop: experiment with stitch widths for different effects.

Stitch length The stitch length should, generally, be closely spaced. If stitches begin to pile up and the fabric becomes difficult to manipulate, try lengthening the stitch.

Preparation Framing is optional, but if the fabric is framed it will be easier to manipulate the work as you sew, producing curves and patterns. Framing is not necessary if you are stitching fairly straight lines.

Machining Sew satin stitch over the tacking foot in any desired pattern. Since these stitches will easily pull out of the fabric, it is necessary to secure them. To achieve this, push the finished loops to one side and sew a very narrow satin stitch over the line where the stitches enter the fabric. Alternatively, place a piece of iron-on interfacing at the back to secure the stitches. To produce a fringe, carefully clip the loops that are formed, or leave the loops as they are for a softer textural effect.

Satin stitch has been worked here with a tailor tacking foot, and the fabric was moved from side to side under the needle to produce flowing curves.

Satin stitch fringe

This is one of the decorative fringes that can be produced by machine. The fringe can be made to a length that is nearly double the width of the satin stitch. It is one of many techniques available to create texture and may be sewn directly to fabric. Alternatively, it may be worked on non-woven interfacing or vanishing muslin to create a strip of fringe that can be applied to any piece of embroidery. Use this stitch on panels and in combination with other techniques. Not all machines will lock on the inner edge at the wrong side, with the top thread covering both sides, and if it is difficult to produce this stitch on your machine, use the fringe stitch described on page 40.

Prepare your machine as for satin stitch edging for shapes. It is imperative, however, that the satin stitch locks on the inner edge of the stitch, on the underside of the fabric, covering both sides of the fabric.

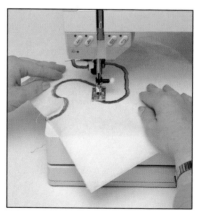

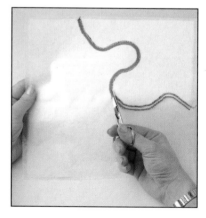

1 Transfer the design to fabric and sew it in satin stitch, following the lines of the design. To produce a thick fringe, set the machine for very close stitches. The width of the stitch will determine the length of the fringe.

2 Turn to the wrong side of the fabric and find the line where the stitches lock. Sew a very narrow line of close satin stitch to cover and secure the locking stitch.

3 With very fine scissors, cut the first, wide satin stitch as close to the narrow satin stitch as possible. Do not cut the narrow satin stitch that covers the locking stitches.

Many rows of satin stitch fringe have been sewn next to each other to build up an area of textured fringe.

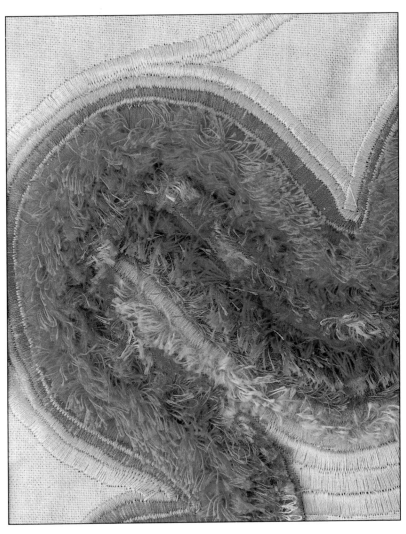

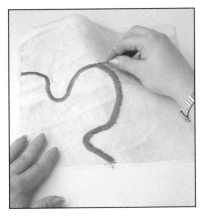

4 Turn to the front of the piece. With the point of a needle, gently pull the clipped ends of the satin stitch through to the front. You will now have a row of fringe nearly twice as long as the width of the wide satin stitch.

43

Satin stitch cords

Cords are produced by sewing satin stitch over a cord or string, so the machine is set up for satin stitch. No fabric is placed under the cord while the satin stitch is being sewn.

Cord Use any heavy string, drapery cord, heavy wool, thread, crochet cotton or wire.

Threads Machine embroidery threads are used, with the same thread in the bobbin as on the top of the machine. Some shiny threads, such as rayon threads, will resist this technique and are thus unsuitable.

Foot Either a general sewing or a zigzag foot may be used. A walking foot is an aid in feeding the cord, but it is not essential.

Tension Set the top tension looser than normal; the bobbin tension should be slightly increased. Threads should lock on the bottom of the cord, allowing the top thread to wrap completely around the cord. Adjust the tension so that the threads are tightly wrapped around the cord.

Stitch length If the stitch length is too closely spaced, stitches may pile up on the cord. If this happens, lengthen the stitch setting. Try to keep stitches as close together as possible without piling up.

Stitch width The stitch must be wider than the diameter of the cord, covering it without sewing into it.

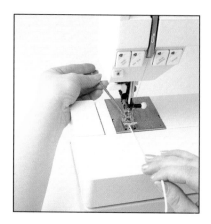

1 **Place the string or cord under the presser foot. Leave a long tail on the cord so that one hand can grip the cord to apply a gentle pulling pressure, assisting the feed dogs along the sewing line. More than one pass through the machine will be necessary to achieve full coverage of the cord.**

2 **Interesting effects may be produced by stitching over soft embroidery threads or wool. Almost any decorative utility stitch can be used to apply interesting patterns, and threads can be bunched to create heavily textured cords.**

Crazy patchwork

Hard-wearing and washable quilts or garments can be produced with this patchwork technique. If you use decorative stitches, you will not need to turn the edges of each piece of fabric under before you join them, as the stitching will hide and secure the raw edges. Decorative stitches can also be used when quilting.

Fabrics The top fabric may be any medium-weight cotton or silk. The background fabric can be medium-weight cotton or, even, a type of blanket fabric. Batting can be used between layers.

Threads Virtually any thread may be used. Select a few spools in shades chosen to coordinate with the colour of the top and background fabrics.

Needle Choose a needle that will accommodate the threads and fabric.

1 Cut a square of background fabric and a few interesting shapes of top fabric. Baste or lightly spray-glue the shapes to the background fabric.

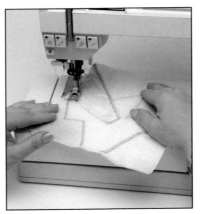

2 Select a decorative stitch and begin stitching. Be sure to cover all cut edges of the top fabric pieces. Vary the stitch length and width as sewing progresses and change thread colour freely.

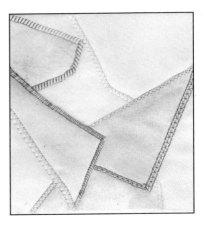

3 Continue to add top fabric shapes, stitching them as before. It does not matter if shapes or stitches overlap each other: let your creative instincts flow and dictate the direction of the growing design.

Foot Use the general sewing presser foot, satin stitch or open toe (appliqué) foot.

Tensions Set the top tension so that the bobbin thread does not show through to the front of the fabric; if it does, slightly loosen the top tension. The bobbin tension should be set for normal sewing.

Stitch width You may choose to vary the stitch width as sewing progresses, in order to provide an additional creative dimension to the work.

Stitch length Again, vary the stitch length at your artistic whim.

4 To ensure that all the squares will unite in a cohesive whole, try to create each one in a similar fashion and with a toning balance of colours: carbon copies are not necessary. If desired, finished squares may then be joined into a larger piece.

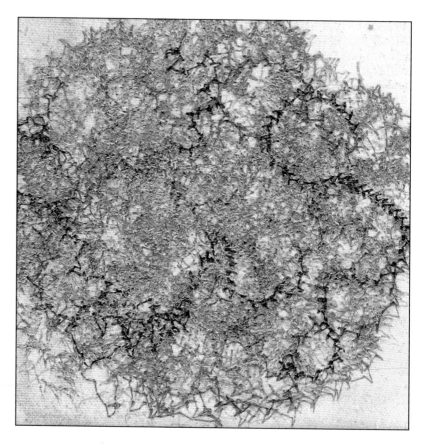

Exploring decorative stitches

Most machine embroiderers tend to dismiss the fixed or programmed decorative stitches as being too traditional for use in creative machine embroidery. But although the stitch may be programmed, the manner in which it is used can express creativity. Programmed stitches, when used with unusual combinations of threads and fabrics, can be the basis of interesting work, especially as many machines allow up to 10 stitch lengths and around 20 stitch widths. These elements allow ample scope for experimentation and individual creativity.

To use decorative stitches free style, frame the fabric and, using the general sewing presser foot, move the frame from side to side. Since the feed dogs are up, it is inadvisable to move the frame backward and forward during sewing. Pivoting the fabric about the needle, without pushing or pulling as in free machining, experiment with a broad selection of stitches in varying widths and lengths. Automatic decorative stitches may be used (*left*) or satin stitch (*right*).

Couched fabric strips

A new fabric may be created by couching torn or cut fabric strips. The technique may be used to embellish clothing or it can be incorporated in a design for a panel or quilt. This is an excellent opportunity to use up scraps or odd pieces of fabric, which can be re-dyed or bleached to change colour and character.

Fabric The background fabric should be of medium or heavy weight, or have a backing attached so that the fabric is stiff enough to support the applied strips and the heavy machine embroidery. The applied fabrics may be of any type and should be torn or cut into strips from 3 to 6mm (⅛ to ¼in.) wide. The colour of the strips should relate to the colour scheme of the background fabric.

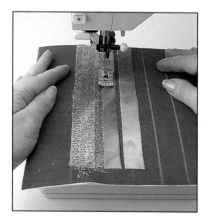

1 Mark a few right angles on the background fabric to ensure that the strips are laid on it in parallel lines, and do not start to run crookedly. Lay strips of fabric on the background, one strip at a time. Alternate different widths of strip with different lengths and widths of decorative stitches. Several rows of stitching may be used to secure each strip.

2 Stitch in parallel rows and occasionally couch a thread or two, blending these in with the general colour scheme. Sew a few rows of satin stitch at random, regardless of any other stitch applied. Let some of the background fabric peek through the fabric strips and stitching.

Thread Again, coordinate colours with the overall scheme. Variegated threads can create very interesting effects.

Needle Choose a needle to suit the size of thread and type of fabric.

Stitch Select an automatic decorative stitch, such as zigzag or one of the more complex options.

Foot Use either the general sewing presser foot, the satin stitch foot or the open toe foot.

Stitch width Vary the stitch width on successive strips.

Stitch length Some machines allow the stitch pattern to be lengthened. If yours has this capacity, vary the stitch length of the decorative pattern on successive strips.

Mirror image Some machines will allow the decorative stitch to be produced in mirror image format. If so, apply this technique as well.

Fabric strips have here been couched to a background with many variations of stitch pattern. (Embroidery by Gail Harker; cushion made by Chris Bentley.)

Cable stitch

Cable stitch is actually a heavy thread couched to a fabric by an ordinary sewing thread. The stitch is made with the underside of the fabric upwards, and the right side of the fabric facing the feed dogs. It is often difficult, on heavy or thick fabric, to create a good outline, as many stitches simply disappear into the fabric: cable stitch not only solves this problem, but does so easily, while using ordinary straight stitch. This stitch is normally used as an outline stitch on velvet, wool, cotton, upholstery or other heavy fabrics. Cable stitch may resemble simple hand couching, and can also be used as a quilting stitch. Since the stitch is worked upside down, the design may be drawn directly on the reverse side of the background fabric.

Fabric Try using heavy-weight cotton, wool, silk, velvet or, perhaps, upholstery fabrics.

Thread For the bobbin thread, use a perlé thread, 6-stranded embroidery thread, or fine knitting or crochet wools. Thread the top of the machine with dressmakers' No. 50. If it is desirable for the couching thread to be unseen, use invisible (nylon) thread.

Needle Begin with a size 90(14) and change if necessary.

Stitch Use straight stitch.

Foot Use the general sewing presser foot.

Tensions The top tension may require no adjustment to form a neat, tight, couching stitch. For most heavy threads, the bobbin tension will normally have to be loosened so that the thicker thread will spool off the bobbin with about the same tension as normal sewing thread.

Stitch length Normal stitch length is generally satisfactory, but experiment for different effects.

Machining Before beginning this stitch, bring the bobbin thread up through the fabric. As machining is begun, check tensions to ensure that a proper stitch is being made. The bobbin thread should lie neatly secured to the fabric with a tight couching stitch.

Cable stitch with quilting

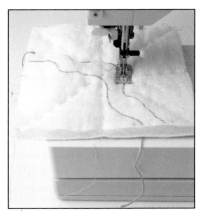

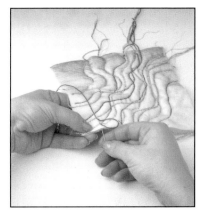

1 Hand baste the three layers – top fabric, batting and muslin backing – securely together. Transfer the design to the back of the fabric.

2 Place the right side of the fabric face down over the feed dogs. Bring the bobbin thread to the surface and begin stitching with straight stitch.

3 Do not backstitch at the beginning of this technique; leave the long tails of the bobbin thread hanging loose; then, using a needle, bring the tails to the wrong side of the fabric and tie them off to finish the piece.

Inspired by the reflection of light on snow, this cotton velvet fabric was first airbrushed with fabric dye, and then quilted, using cable stitch.

CHAPTER 3

FREE MACHINE EMBROIDERY

Free machine embroidery opens the door to a whole new world of artistic expression. Try to visualize the needle as a pencil or a paint brush: moving your framed piece of fabric under the needle is like drawing on a sheet of paper or painting on a canvas. Free running stitch, zigzag and some of the automatic stitches will produce lines of wide, narrow or variable width, and textures from an enormous palette of coloured threads. The movement of the framed fabric is within the full control of the artist.

Ensure that the machine is sewing properly – in other words that stitches are forming correctly and are not being skipped – and that tensions are set for general sewing. If not, adjust your machine for the perfect straight stitch (see page 16). It is usually easier for the inexperienced to begin with a machine adjusted in the automatic mode. However, as one gains experience and acquires a feel for the adjustments, simply set your machine up for free running stitch (see below) immediately, without this preliminary stage.

As you become more experienced you will be able to stop using the embroidery frame. Try stiffening your fabric by using a roller blind stiffener. This can be bought as a spray or a liquid, which needs to be diluted with water. Alternatively, layer a few pieces of fabric and baste them together. Place your hands on either side of the needle to support the fabric: you can then move the fabric in any direction.

It is important to start by adjusting your machine for automatic stitching. After this, the transition to free machine embroidery will require only minor adjustments. In both modes of operation, the presser bar must be lowered while sewing. Always return the tensions to the normal settings after using either mode.

Persian Pot of Flowers, by Margaret Hall, represents an attempt to create an embroidery with a rich, mysterious, oriental atmosphere and an icon-like quality.

Setting-up for free running stitch

Free running stitch (also called straight stitch) is the basis for most free machine embroidery. The most effective method is to maintain a fairly high machine running speed. Too low a running speed can result in needle breakage, drag on the fabric, skipped stitches, or stitches too closely spaced.

It is better to move the frame at a rate that does not allow too much thread to build up on the fabric. Practise lines, circles or curves. Move the frame rhythmically, avoiding jerks and rapid movements.

Fabrics Use medium- to heavy-weight cotton. Lighter fabrics should be backed with a layer of fabric or interfacing.

Threads Any machine embroidery thread may be used on the top of the machine. Use machine embroidery cotton thread or dressmakers' No. 50 in the bobbin. Do not use No. 40 dressmakers' cotton for free machine embroidery.

Needle Use a size 90(14) needle – this breaks less readily and is good for practice.

Foot Start by experimenting without a foot, lowering the presser bar and removing the foot altogether. If you find it difficult to sew without a foot, attach the darning foot.

Stitch length Set the stitch length to '0', to stop the feed dogs moving. The stitch length setting controls the back-and-forth movement of the feed dogs. Although the feed dogs are lowered, any movement may still snag the threads or fabric. If you cannot set your machine at '0', select the lowest possible number.

Stitch width Set the stitch width to '0'.

Tensions Adjust tensions as for the perfect stitch. If the perfect stitch cannot be achieved on your machine, it is better to have a bit of the top thread showing on the bottom of the fabric, than for the bobbin thread to show through on the front.

Preparation Lower or cover the feed dogs. Ensure that the material is tightly framed in an embroidery frame.

1 Lower the presser bar, as if lowering the foot. Bring both threads to the surface of the machine.

2 Begin to stitch, moving the frame in any direction. By coordinating the movement of the frame and speed of sewing with the foot pedal, you will be able to control the size, length and direction of stitch.

Textured stitches based on free running stitch

Many patterns can be developed from free running stitch, and these can be further developed in many different ways – to fill in a design, to secure collages of fabric and thread, for appliqué and quilting – the design possibilities are endless. After you have experimented with some of the stitch patterns shown here, it might be fun to sketch out some ideas of your own, using pencil and paper.

Early machine embroiderers used granite, or seed, stitch (left-hand side of the picture), in which circles overlap.

Vermicelli, or crazy, stitch (right-hand side) is another of the popular patterns used to cover large areas of fabric. The pattern is worked in a series of half circles.

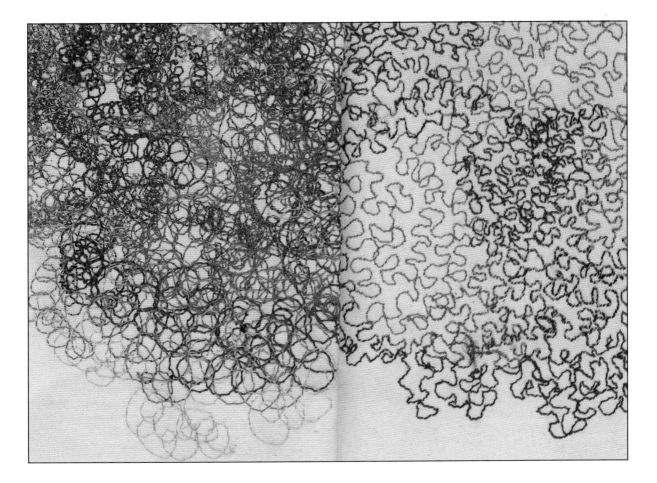

Drawing with the needle

Drawing with the needle is similar to putting pencil to paper or brush to canvas. You can freely sketch by eye or follow designs that have been previously applied to the fabric, and the free running stitch may be used both as an outline stitch and as a filling stitch. Although you cannot shade colours in exactly the same way as in a painting, you can achieve subtle effects by using shaded threads, or by stitching over the same area with different colours, so that they overlap and mingle with each other.

Once you have acquired the ability to draw with the needle, you can mix stitches and techniques, allowing your creative instincts to decide the direction that your work should take. You might, for

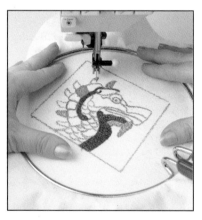

1 Take the piece of fabric to be embroidered, cutting it to the size of the finished design plus a margin for framing. Cut a piece of light-weight iron-on Vilene the same size and lay it over the design, fusible side down. If you cannot see the design clearly, use a lightbox or tape the design and Vilene to a window. Trace the design onto the Vilene.

2 Fuse the Vilene with the design traced on it to the right side of the fabric, following the manufacturer's instructions. Cut a second piece of Vilene, the same size as the first, and apply it to the back of the fabric.

3 Frame the fabric tightly and set your machine for free running stitch. Begin sewing and move the frame to create the desired effect. Work some straight lines, so that they overlap, meet each other and so on. Work small sections at a time, filling in background areas to suit the design.

4 The fabric will become very heavy with thread. If difficulty in sewing with the foot off is ever a problem with your machine, it will probably be encountered with this technique. If so, try using the darning foot. A clear plastic darning foot is particularly helpful, enabling you to see the stitching as it is applied to the design.

example, try making your own background fabric, or you could dye or quilt the background, and for the embroidery itself you might choose to combine machine work with hand stitches.

It is advisable to use a firm, heavy cotton or upholstery fabric, which will be easy to stitch. If your chosen fabric is relatively light-weight, it may be necessary to stiffen the fabric by backing it with additional fabric, interfacing, or heavy fusible interlining. Ensure that you leave a sufficient border of unworked fabric around the design to allow for framing.

Prepare your machine in the same way as for free running stitch. Use the smallest frame that is practical and the smallest needle that will accommodate the thread and fabric.

Free zigzag stitch

Frame the fabric and set your machine up as for free running stitch; the only exception will be the stitch width, which can be set at whatever suits your purpose. To accomplish complete coverage of the fabric by the top thread, you may require a slight reduction in top tension. It is advisable to use a heavy fabric or one that has been backed with an interfacing. The frame can be moved in any direction as you work. If you move the frame slowly, while applying full power to the foot pedal, a satin stitch will be produced. If the frame is moved more quickly and less power is applied through the foot pedal, an open zigzag can be produced.

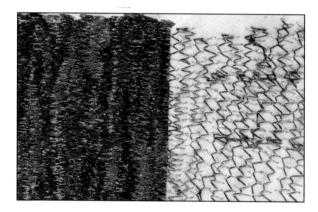

Free zigzag stitch (left) has been worked with a wide stitch width and the frame moved very fast. The stitches become more dense when the frame is moved more slowly. The gold bobbin thread is seen on the surface of the fabric.

In this sample (bottom left), free zigzag stitch was worked as the frame was moved with a circular motion.

Satin stitch beads (below) are made by working satin stitches closely together.

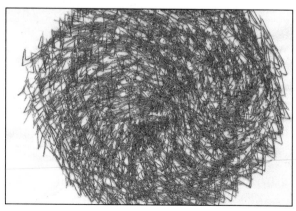

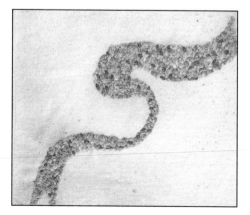

Satin stitch beads

Satin stitch beads can be densely packed together or spaced further apart. A thread, which may be left as it is or clipped, will run between each bead. Place the framed fabric under the needle; then lower the presser bar and select the preferred stitch width. Begin stitching, but hold the frame in place. A bead of built-up satin stitch will begin to form. When the bead reaches the desired size, raise the presser bar; move to the next position, and continue the process. Do not allow the build-up to clog the machine.

If it is desirable to clip the connecting threads, a few stitches, made with the width setting set at '0', will secure the thread at the beginning and end of each bead.

In Winter Flowers *free zigzag stitch was worked from side to side on canvas. The petals were cut away and free running stitch was worked across the open areas. No frame was used for this work.*

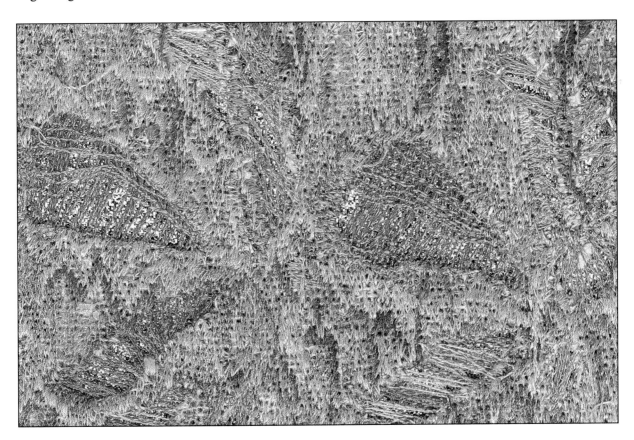

Free machine quilting

Free machine quilting gives one the freedom to create beautiful, flowing lines that are not possible with automatic quilting. You can use running stitches, as in most quilting, or you may choose to incorporate any of the textured stitches, creating an even greater relief on the surface fabric. Do not despair while learning this technique: you may need a fair amount of practice before you achieve a rhythm that creates nice, even stitches on quilted fabric, but the results will justify the time and effort.

Fabrics These are basically the same three layers as for automatic quilting (see page 32), except that for free machine quilting the fabrics should normally be held in a frame, which will limit the thickness of batting that can be used. It is, however, possible to frame fabrics and batting of reasonable thickness. If the fabric layers are thick and firm, framing may not be necessary.

In this work by Annwyn Dean, free machine quilting is used for a design inspired by machinery.

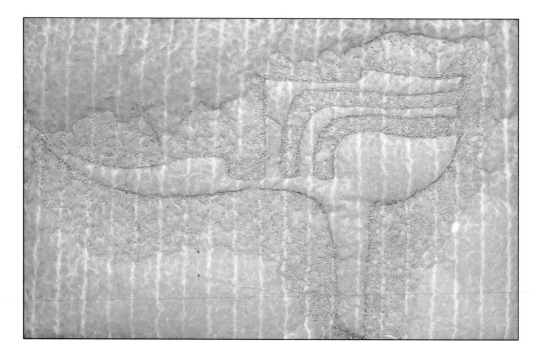

Threads Most embroidery threads may be used as may ordinary sewing thread. Contrast or coordinate the thread colour with that of the top fabric.

Needle Match the needle to the fabric and the size of thread.

Stitches Free running and zigzag stitches are acceptable for quilting. Experiment with different fabrics and threads to find harmonious combinations.

Preparation Prepare the piece for quilting by basting the layers together, starting from the centre and working out to the edges, as for automatic machine quilting.

Alternatively, a very light application of spray glue may be used to bond the layers together.

Machining Remove the general sewing foot from the presser bar (if you encounter sewing difficulties, attach the darning foot). Lower the feed dogs.

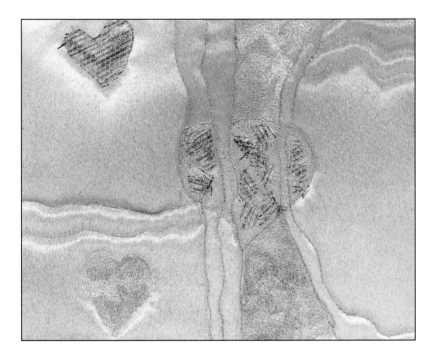

In Broken Hearts II, *some of the quilting was done in free running stitch. Free running seed stitch was used to create further relief, and the appliquéd fabric pieces were attached with free running stitch.*

Free machine quilting with trapunto

Trapunto is a technique characterized by selective padding of different areas. Using free machine quilting to create curved and wandering lines, areas may be isolated, allowing the addition of extra padding for a much more sculptured effect.

Prepare your machine as for free machine quilting.

Fabrics For the top fabric, try using soft, shiny fabric such as silk or cotton sateen. Some velvets will take on a dramatic appearance with this technique.

Any standard batting can be used for the filling. For an interesting effect, use a transparent top fabric and fill the quilted areas with coloured threads, wools, scraps of fabric or any material that will produce the subtle colours desired.

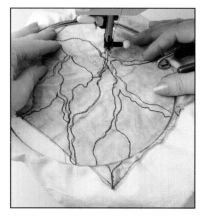

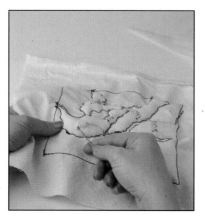

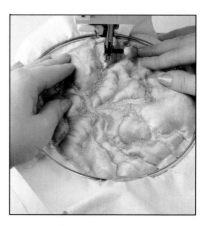

1 Transfer the design to the top fabric and baste the top and bottom fabrics together. Frame the work, then use free running stitch to sew over the design outlines. When the design is fully retraced, remove basting.

2 Turn to the wrong side of the work and – for small shapes on open-weave fabric – use a knitting needle to part the fabric, then fill the area with the desired filling material. To fill larger shapes, cut the backing material at the centre of the area; insert batting, and overcast the opening.

3 Free running stitch may be applied over the top fabric after the batting has been inserted. This will add stitchery interest and give a more sculptured look to the piece.

Silver leather was used as the base for Ice in Canadian Winter. *Sheer fabric was then free machined onto the base. The channels were filled with coloured threads and batting. Some areas were cut away, and the surface was further quilted with free running stitch.*

For the bottom fabric, use any light- to medium-weight cotton, such as muslin or scrim. If you use a very fine, open, loosely-woven fabric, you can gently part the threads to insert the filling, without having to make a slit.

You might also like to create your own, original top fabric for use with trapunto.

Stitch Use free running stitch.

Couched threads with loops

Free machining techniques can easily be used for couching threads. These may be arranged in loops or other designs and may be of any length. Almost any type of thread can be used, as can cord, ribbon, fabric strips, string or knitting wool. The (top) sewing thread is not intended to be seen and should therefore be the same colour as the couched thread. The bobbin thread may be any thread of your choice.

Stitches Free running stitch or free zigzag.

Foot Use the darning foot, or sew without a foot.

Preparation The background fabric should be framed for this technique. Paper or other interfacing may be used to provide additional stiffness if required.

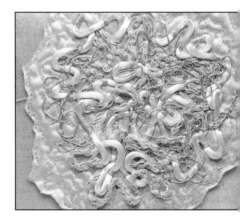

An example of couched cords applied at random and embellished with satin stitch beads.

1 Draw with a pencil or transfer a design to the top fabric. Form a loop of the thread that is to be couched. With the left index finger, hold the loop on the top fabric and stitch over the protruding ends to the right of the finger. Continue this process, forming loops as required.

2 Continue to add loops until the desired amount of build-up is accomplished. This is not continuous stitching, but a start-stop process as each loop is formed and attached. Make small stitches over the edges of the couched thread. It is important to ensure that the loops are close together in order to get even coverage.

Eyelets

Eyelets are traditionally the basis of broderie anglaise, but with free machining you can expand upon this conventional use, creating wonderful clusters of textured motifs, perhaps with eyelets of different sizes combined on one fabric.

Eyelets may be used in many creative ways: they may be overlapped and varied in size or shape, or small roundels may be cut from fabric and glued or basted to the background fabric in random patterns. You can punch holes through both fabrics to create raised eyelets, though if the roundels are cut from very thick fabric, the eyelet stud may not engage the fabric.

When the satin stitch is applied to the roundels, it creates the eyelet as well as attaching the roundel, which may protrude beyond the satin stitch. You can create interesting textures and patterns with roundels and it is well worth experimenting with different fabrics.

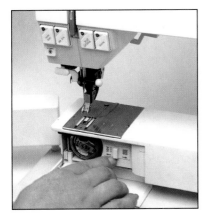 

1 Remove the presser foot and lower the feed dogs. Secure the eyelet plate over the feed dogs. Frame the fabric tightly with a small frame, about 8 to 9 cm (3¼ to 3¾in.) in diameter, unless heavy fabric such as pelmet Vilene or belting is being used.

2 Punch a small hole in the fabric with a pointed instrument, and position the hole over the eyelet stud. Lower the presser bar and adjust the stitch width. Begin stitching, while pivoting the fabric about the eyelet stud. Check your machine manual for any special instructions for your machine.

Eyelets with a plate

There are several variations on this technique, but it is best to start with the comparatively conventional method outlined here. Prepare for machining by fitting in the eyelet plate and – unless the fabric is very stiff – by setting the work in a frame.

Threads Use any machine embroidery thread.

Stitch Use satin stitch throughout.

Foot Remove the foot.

Tension You may find that it is necessary to adjust the bobbin tension in order to ensure that no bobbin thread is visible on the right side.

Eyelets without a plate

Do not throw up your hands in despair if you do not have an eyelet plate; this attachment will, in any case, produce only one size of eyelet. The following instructions will enable you to make eyelets of any size.

Start by preparing your machine as already described, but do not use the eyelet plate. Use a firm fabric, held in a small frame, and draw on the fabric an eyelet of the required size and shape. Using free running stitch, stitch two or three times around the border of the shape to strengthen the edge. Remove the fabric from the frame. With small, sharp scissors, carefully cut a hole inside the stitched area and re-frame the fabric. Set the stitch width at the desired setting and carefully stitch round the hole, pivoting about the centre of the hole as sewing progresses. Finish stitching on the outer edge of the eyelet; take the top thread to the back, and tie it off.

You may find it easier to stitch if you place a piece of paper interfacing under the eyelet, tearing it away when you have finished.

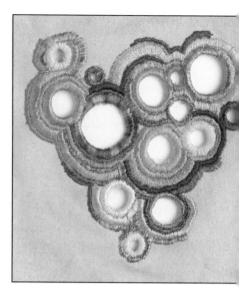

This sample shows large eyelets, made without the use of an eyelet plate.

Whip stitch

Whip stitch is a raised stitch that intentionally shows only the bobbin thread on the surface of the fabric. The top of the machine is threaded with a heavy thread and the top tension is increased; as a result, the bobbin thread is pulled up through the fabric and whips around the top thread, creating a beautiful 'looped' effect. Whip stitch requires very slow movement of the frame.

Fabric Use a firm fabric, tightly framed in a small embroidery frame.

Threads For the top thread, use ordinary dressmakers' cotton thread No. 40 or No. 50. Alternatively, two threads can be used simultaneously; though you may need to fit a special topstitching needle to prevent the threads from shredding.

For the bobbin thread, finest machine embroidery thread is ideal, but some machines will accommodate metallic threads, rayons and mixtures.

Needle Use a size 90(14), or choose a needle to suit the thread and fabric.

Foot Remove the foot, but use a darning foot if it proves difficult to stitch without a foot.

Tensions Increase the top tension in small steps until the bobbin thread is visible on the surface of the fabric. This will be tighter than

The three samples below show feather stitch, a variation on whip stitch (see page 69).

Bottom left *Feather stitch has been worked on net, using a loose bobbin tension so that the bobbin thread shows on the surface of the net.*

Centre *Feather stitch has been worked on cotton muslin – a circular movement creates lace holes.*

Bottom *For basic feather stitch, the frame is moved in a circular motion, more quickly than for whip stitch. A tight top tension and loose bobbin tension draws the bobbin thread to the surface.*

1 *Lightning Strikes Twice* was selected as the design theme for this piece. To translate the feeling of lightning and dark skies, small shapes were torn, cut, and glued to a sheet of paper, and this arrangement of shapes and colours became the design for the finished embroidery.

2 Using cotton fabric dye, following the manufacturer's instructions, the design was painted on the background fabric. The dye transferred the design to the background fabric and provides the background colour where the fabric peeks through the stitches.

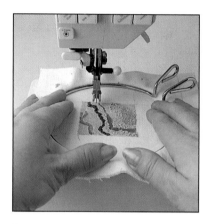

3 The machine was prepared for whip stitch and the tightly-framed fabric was positioned under the needle. The frame was moved very slowly, with the foot pedal depressed so that the machine ran very fast. Rows of bobbin thread, forming in loops, appeared on the surface.

for 'normal' sewing. Normal sewing tension will, usually, be indicated by a number on the dial between '3' and '5', or by a coloured line. Tension adjustment could go as high as '9'. If the top thread breaks, reduce tension. Decrease the bobbin tension so that it is slightly less than for 'normal' sewing. Some machines allow bobbin tension to be bypassed – read your manual.

Tension adjustment for this technique is all important. On some machines, high top tension will result in continual breakage of the top thread. If this occurs, reduce the bobbin tension slightly. If the finished stitch is irregular or lumpy, either the top tension is not set tightly enough or the bobbin tension is too tight, so readjust tensions.

Some machines with drop-in bobbins do not permit the required degree of low tension. This condition may be compensated by the use of a heavier thread on the top or by wrapping the top thread, once or twice, around a second spool pin on the top of the machine.

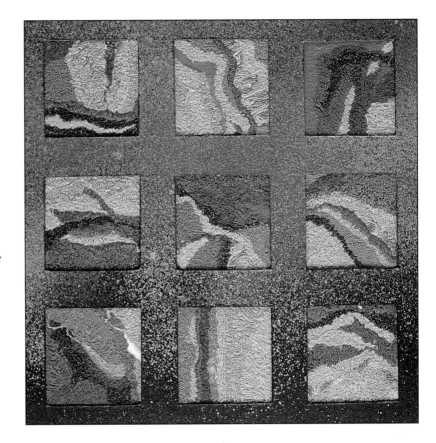

The finished piece, Lightning Strikes Twice, *is composed of nine patches, each approximately 4.5cm (1³/₄in.) square. The background fabric is dyed cotton twill.*

Preparation Prepare your machine as for free machine embroidery, by lowering or covering the feed dogs and removing the foot altogether or fitting the darning foot.

Variations on whip stitch

Whip stitch is one of the few stitches that places great strain on the top tension. Each machine reacts a little differently to the next, and only by experimenting will you discover the possibilities of the stitch on your machine. Feather stitch is a variation of whip stitch: follow directions for whip stitch, but increase the top tension to the maximum, reduce the bobbin tension to the minimum and move the frame more quickly in a circular fashion.

Free cable stitch

Free cable stitch is used to create a high, three-dimensional, textured build-up of heavy threads on fabric. This is accomplished through the use of hand-embroidery threads, wound on the bobbin and applied with the fabric right side down. The obvious difficulty is that you cannot see the progressive build-up of threads. It is therefore necessary to draw the design on the reverse side of the fabric so that you can follow the design lines during sewing. It is advisable to try an experimental piece to ensure that tensions are properly adjusted to achieve the desired result. This experimental piece can also be used to try out different threads.

Fabrics Experiment with a variety of fabrics, including cotton, velvet, organdie, organza, and other unusual types. Ensure that the fabric is tightly framed.

Threads The top thread may be dressmakers' thread, size 50, or machine embroidery thread.

For the bobbin, use hand embroidery threads, perlé, 6-stranded threads, fine knitting and crochet yarns. Try some of the new and exciting combinations of metallic and twisted threads. To wind the bobbin, unroll a length of thread from the ball or skein, but do not cut it until the bobbin is full. Use the bobbin winding mechanism on the machine, but use your fingers as an extra thread guide to ensure that the thread winds on the bobbin evenly. This will prevent sewing problems later. Do not overfill the bobbin.

Needle Choose a needle to suit the thread and fabric.

Stitch Use free running stitch, working in any direction. For a heavy build-up of texture, overlap the stitches.

Tension Adjust tensions as for couched threads. Most heavy threads will require a decrease in bobbin tension, which should be adjusted so that the heavy thread spools off at about the same rate as normal sewing thread. For a loose, looping stitch, the bobbin tension can be set very low. Some machines will have a tension bypass for very loopy cable stitch.

The top tension may require some adjustment to ensure a neat, tight couching stitch. This adjustment of top tension secures the bobbin thread to the fabric. Start at normal tension, and increase as required.

Variations with cable stitch

Try increasing the top tension until a suitable amount of bobbin thread is visible on the surface of the fabric. In this variation, the finished side of the fabric may be up.

Alternatively, decrease the top tension below normal, until the top thread is visible on the wrong side of the work.

For Lilac Time, *six-stranded cotton was used in the bobbin. Approximately six shades of purple and green were used to give a depth of colour. Heavy stitching was worked in the foreground until a dense build-up of colour and texture was achieved.*

Free cutwork with lace filling

Cutwork is a traditional hand embroidery technique, in which parts of the background fabric are cut away and filled with lace, with satin stitch worked around the edges of the cut. Generally, closely-woven fabrics, such as cotton, linen or organdie, were used. The most imitative technique is done in the automatic mode, using satin stitch. The technique described here uses free running stitch and lace insertion.

Fabric It is best to use a closely woven fabric that does not fray easily. Try organdie, nylon organza or cotton, and frame the work tightly in a small frame of 12 to 14cm (5 to 6in.) in diameter.

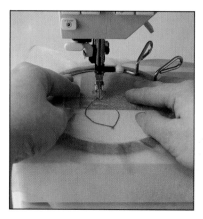

1 Plan a design with a series of shapes to be cut. If you keep the shapes small, the fabric is less likely to be distorted by the embroidery; something worth bearing in mind, especially if a number of cut-outs are to be made. Frame the fabric and set your machine for free running stitch. Stitch around the outline of each shape.

2 Remove the fabric from the frame. With very sharp scissors, carefully cut away the inside area of the shape, cutting close to the stitching. Reframe the fabric and sew a decorative stitch around the edge of the cut-out: seed stitch has been used in this example.

3 Depress the foot pedal for a very fast sewing speed and move the frame from side to side across the open shape. The fast sewing speed will ensure that both the top and bobbin threads twist evenly together as stitches cross the open area. Continue until the desired density is achieved.

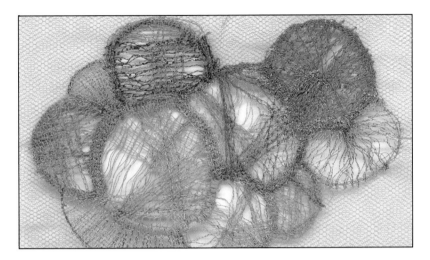

A sample shows lace filling worked on two layers of net.

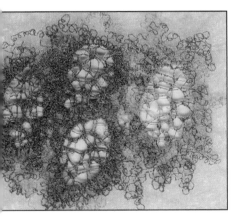

4 After the open area has been covered with stitches to the desired density, try stitching swirls or other patterns on the framework of threads. Continue stitching until the desired effect is achieved, and then move on to the next shape, repeating the process.

Threads Use machine embroidery threads for both the top and the bobbin. Some shiny threads may resist crossing open spaces. If the threads are not of the same size, it may be necessary to adjust the top and/or bobbin tensions. Adjust the tensions until the top thread does not show on the bottom of the fabric and the bobbin thread does not show on the top.

Needle Use any needle that will penetrate the fabric without snagging.

Stitch Use free running stitch.

Tension Unless you are using two different weights of thread (see above), the bobbin tension should be normal and the top tension should be decreased slightly.

You will also require a very sharp pair of embroidery scissors.

Variations on free cutwork with lace filling

Try a wide variety of cut-out shapes. After outlining a shape with stitching, any number of patterns may be used to cross the empty areas. When the shape is filled, satin stitch may be applied to the outline, using either free or automatic satin stitch (automatic stitching is usually easier for the beginner).

The lace cutwork filling may be accomplished without the use of a frame if a stiff fabric like pelmet Vilene or canvas is used.

Open work

Open work lends itself to some very creative machine-embroidery designs. The technique is used with fabrics, from very coarse to fine, that have a very open weave; typical fabrics would be gauze, cheesecloth, scrim, linen and hessian. The loose weave of these kinds of fabric allows the needle to alternately catch one thread (weft or warp), skip to another, and draw them together, creating an open space resembling a buttonhole or eyelet.

The technique may be used where a slashed opening in the fabric is made. The slashed area is then stitched around the edges, drawing two or three threads together to create large open areas in the design.

Feathers were trapped between two layers of nylon organza to make Snow Queen Cape. Free cutwork with lace filling was used, in addition to free running stitch. Twenty shades of machine embroidery thread were used.

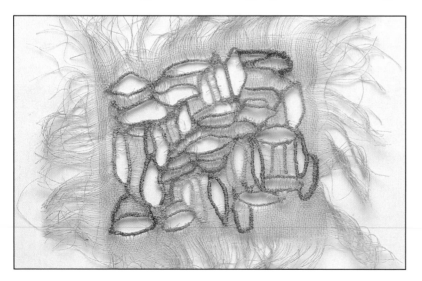

This sample shows open work on linen scrim. The first slit was cut in the fabric and filled with zigzag stitch, after which anothr slit was cut, and so on.

Threads Use machine embroidery threads for both the top and bobbin. If viscose or metallic threads are used on the top, use cotton, machine embroidery thread in the bobbin.

Tension Decrease the top tension slightly. Try normal tension for the bobbin, but you may need to increase the tension slightly.

Machining

For fabrics like hessian or burlap, free zigzag or satin stitch may be used. Set the stitch sufficiently wide to catch two or three threads on each stitch – as the stitching proceeds, the fabric threads will draw tightly together.

On finer, more closely-woven fabrics, such as cheesecloth or gauze, much finer designs are possible: circular shapes are easier to accommodate; the fabric may be slashed in any direction, and free running stitch is easier to work on close weaves. Do not slash more than one or two areas before stitching.

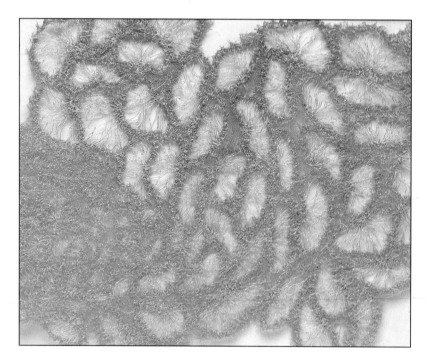

Open work on very fine cotton muslin has been worked with a free running stitch. T-shapes were cut in the fabric, and the spaces were filled.

Drawn-thread work

Traditional drawn-thread work involves the removal, or 'drawing', of threads from the fabric. This leaves areas with threads running in only one direction. The machine embroiderer may then use satin stitch to pull groups of these threads together to resemble handwork, though it is possible to add other machine or hand stitches.

Determine the area from which the threads will be drawn: either warp or weft may be drawn. Withdraw the threads to the edges of the area. On a purely decorative piece, the threads may be cut and discarded.

Fabrics Use an evenweave fabric, such as linen, with threads strong enough to be drawn. Other suitable fabrics are listed under Open work (see pages 74–6).

For this sample, closely woven canvas was put in a frame, threads were withdrawn, and free satin stitch was used to bind groups of threads together.

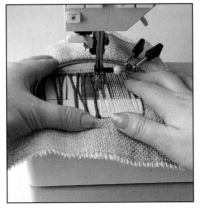

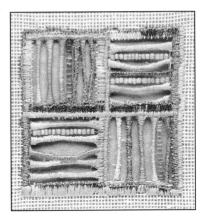

1 Mark out the area for the drawn-thread work. Machine stitch around this area. Cut threads running in one direction, at both ends, and remove them. This will leave a row of threads, all running in the same direction. Frame the fabric.

2 Prepare your machine for free machine embroidery, satin stitch. Work the satin stitch over a group of threads. It is possible to move the frame and pick up other threads as sewing progresses. Edges may be left as they are or finished in satin stitch, with your machine set in the automatic mode.

SPECIAL EFFECTS

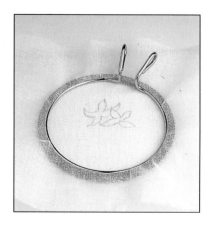

There are numerous special effects that are available only to the machine embroiderer. Both automatic and free machine embroidery techniques, combined with special fabrics, offer endless creative possibilities for the embroiderer.

Lace on vanishing muslin

Beautiful lace effects may be created through the use of a special material called vanishing muslin. Vanishing muslin is a stiffened material that disappears when it is heated with an iron. Either straight or circular stitching patterns may be used. Because zigzag stitches are much looser than straight stitches, it is best to select a

1 Place vanishing muslin in an embroidery frame. Be gentle – the muslin is quite fragile and will not withstand tight stretching in the frame.

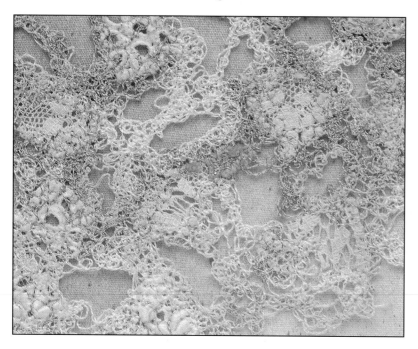

Very small pieces of lace were laid on vanishing muslin and secured with spray glue. Free running stitch was then used to make patterns.

2 Begin sewing with a free stitch that can be intertwined to create a lacy effect. After stitching is completed, trim the excess vanishing muslin close to the embroidery.

3 Place a thin pressing cloth over the stitching and press with a hot, dry iron until the muslin turns a grey brown. The vanishing muslin rapidly deteriorates with the application of heat. Gently remove the ash using a soft toothbrush to clear away stubborn pieces.

4 The finished lace may be used as it is, appliquéd, or starched and formed into three-dimensional shapes.

very narrow stitch width setting and to intersect the lines of stitching frequently if you are using zigzag.

Frame An embroidery frame is recommended.

Threads You can use any natural-fibre thread, such as cotton, cotton perlé, silk or wool. For heavy lace, use crochet cotton or perlé cotton in the bobbin. Synthetic threads are sometimes sensitive to a hot iron, but some may be used in the oven-heat method (see below), and some metallic and shiny threads may be suitable: experiment when in doubt.

Needle Use any needle that is large enough to carry the thread without shredding it.

Colours Try threads in many shades of a few coordinated colours.

Tensions Adjust tensions to form as perfect a free running stitch as possible.

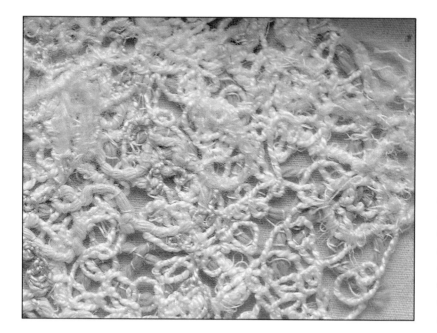

For this sample of free cable stitch lace, perlé hand embroidery thread and knitting cotton were used in the bobbin case. The bobbin tension was loosened. Machine embroidery thread was used on the top. The reverse side of the vanishing muslin is the finished side of the work.

Machining Stitch over a wide area, building up a supporting network over the pattern; then go back over the network to fill in spaces. Do not work stitches too densely in one area until the network is laid down or you may tear the muslin. Move the frame evenly and rhythmically while applying stitches. After all the stitching is applied, cut away the excess muslin, trimming close to the pattern.

Burning away muslin Place a thin pressing cloth over the work. Press with a dry, hot iron until the muslin turns a brown colour. Brush away the dissolved muslin, gently using a soft tooth brush or nail brush to work the remaining pieces of muslin out of the stitching.

Alternative The vanishing muslin may also be removed by heating it in an oven. Pre-heat the oven to 150°C/300°F. Wrap the work in a sheet of foil and place it in the oven for five to six minutes. The muslin will turn a brown colour and gentle rubbing will cause it to disintegrate. As with the ironing method, stubborn pieces can be removed with a brush. Do not be tempted to leave the embroidery in the oven for a longer period of time.

Free machine lace on cold-water-soluble fabric

Cold-water-soluble fabric is a spun alginate, woven into sheets that have the look and feel of thin plastic sheeting. This fabric can be embroidered in the same way as vanishing muslin. However, only machine embroidery threads are recommended for this technique, because larger, thicker threads have a tendency to split the fabric. The fabric can be used to produce very fine, delicate lace.

While the manufacturers recommend dissolving the fabric in cold water, experience indicates that warm, soapy water, followed by a cold rinse, is an effective way of removing the soluble fabric. After removing the soluble fabric, lay the piece of lace on a towel to dry, blocking if necessary. Starch may be applied to the piece if it is to form a three-dimensional shape.

Needle To suit the thread: if problems are encountered, try a ballpoint needle.

Stitch Use free running stitch only: zigzag stitches will tear the fabric.

Stitch length Ensure that the stitch length is set at '0': even though the feed dogs are down, they will move and may come into contact with the fabric, tearing holes, unless you take this precaution.

Variations on cold-water-soluble fabric

Lay a single layer of soluble fabric on a work surface. On the fabric, lay small pieces of lace, net, transparent fabrics, bundles of thread and so on: a trace of spray glue applied to each piece will help to secure them temporarily. Place a top layer of soluble fabric over the pieces to create a 'sandwich' of materials. Frame the sandwich and, treating it as one piece of fabric, machine free running stitch over it, being careful to intertwine the stitches to create a supporting network. The soluble fabric is very fragile and is easily split, so it is important to avoid dense stitches and stitching in one spot. Be sure to hold the fabric close to the flat bed of the machine while stitching, keeping the foot pedal depressed.

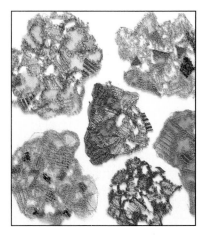

For these samples, various pieces of fabric, lace, ribbon and net were laid on a background of cold-water-soluble fabric. Another layer of cold-water-soluble fabric was placed on top. The layers were then placed in a frame and free running stitch was used to stitch them together.

Lace and other textured fabrics on hot-water-soluble fabric

Hot-water-soluble fabric is much sturdier than cold-water-soluble fabric, and can take much more dense stitching and added layers of other fabrics. The fabric may be worked both framed and without a frame, and cable stitch may be applied. If you work without a frame you will need to set your machine for automatic stitching with the sewing foot on. Zigzag stitches may be applied, but be sure to stitch over the zigzag with two or three lines of straight running stitch or the zigzag will unravel when the fabric is dissolved.

After the stitches have been applied, place the work in a pan of gently boiling (simmering) water for about five minutes or until the fabric is dissolved. The work will appear to be shrivelled up, but do not despair. Rinse under warm flowing water. After rinsing, lay the work on a dry towel and gently stretch and shape the piece, leaving it to dry naturally.

Automatic stitches were used to make lace on hot-water-soluble fabric: net was laid over the fabric and was decorated with straight and zigzag stitches. A frame was not used. The technique can result in a slight shrinkage of threads, which can be very attractive.

Beads and sequins

Applying beads and sequins by machine will come as a great relief to anyone who has had the tedious task of applying them by hand. Tiny beads strung on a thread may be applied by free machine techniques. If they can be purchased pre-strung, all the better. If not, thread them with a beading needle. Sometimes, pre-strung beads may be on a weak thread. If that happens, re-string them by tying a transparent nylon thread to one end of the existing string and gently pushing the beads to the new thread.

Fabric Any fabric may be used.

Thread Use invisible nylon for the top thread. For the bobbin, use machine embroidery cotton or No. 50 dressmakers' cotton.

Foot No foot is used. Remove the foot-attaching fitting from the presser bar if it is obstructing the beads.

Tension Decrease the top tension slightly; set the bobbin tension at normal.

Machining Transfer or draw the chosen design on the fabric. Lay the strings of beads over the design, as desired, and pin over the strings to hold them in place. Remove pins as you sew and do not stitch over them.

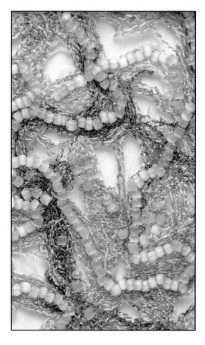

To make this sample, beads and sequins were free-machined onto hot-water-soluble fabric.

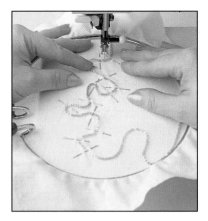

Frame the fabric and set your machine for free running stitch. Sew on the spot to secure the thread, and stitch alongside the string of beads, moving the frame from side to side, so that the top thread falls between each bead. The beads will need to be held in position by hand, so watch your fingers.

The beads tend to deflect the needle, but straight running stitch will fasten them very securely. Sequins may be attached in the same way.

Layering

One of the most innovative and rewarding techniques available to machine embroiderers is the creation of fabrics. Layering fabrics is a technique that may be used to create individual pieces of great variety in texture, pattern and colour. Fabrics are not the only materials that may be captured between layers. Rich colours and textures may be created through the addition of threads, beads, cords, ribbons, feathers, twigs and other odds and ends, held between layers of fabric. Select a heavy, cotton fabric for the background material.

Fabrics and oddments to layer Select any fabric that attracts you, for example shiny or transparent fabrics, unusual weaves, nylon, cotton, velvet or satin. Add strings of beads, satin stitch cords, hand and machine embroidery threads, lace, or whatever is available.

Needle Use a size 90(14) or 100(16), or choose a needle to suit the thread and fabric.

Stitches Incorporate free machine stitches, such as free running stitch, zigzag, or satin stitches.

Foot Try stitching with no foot: if problems occur, use the darning foot.

Tensions Refer to free running stitch.

Preparation Frame the background material unless it is sufficiently stiff to allow free machining without being framed. Arrange small pieces of fabric on the background material. A bit of spray glue or fusible interfacing – follow manufacturers' instructions – will help to hold pieces in place. Lay any threads or cords on the background. Build up textures and colours, in layers, on the background.

When you are satisfied that the layers make a pleasing combination of colour and texture, stitch over them, either at random or in any selected design or pattern.

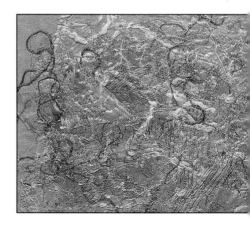

Pieces of fabric, hand embroidery threads and plastic film were laid on the background fabric. Free running stitch and zigzag, in neutral colours, were stitched over the pieces to blend them together.

Layering and cutwork

One fabric creation technique involves layering irregularly shaped pieces of near-transparent fabric. A design is stitched into the fabric, creating enclosed shapes. Material is then cut from within these shapes, and various layers are selectively cut away, creating subtle shapes and changes of colour. A free cable stitch is then worked around the edges of the shape.

You can, if you choose, work spontaneously rather than from a pre-determined pattern. Use free-flowing shapes, squares, circles, wavering lines, or whatever strikes your fancy.

Fabric layers To prepare the foundation fabric, first cut a piece of muslin slightly larger than the finished piece will be. Place on the muslin a layer of batting. Add the background fabric, which should be a medium- to heavy-weight cotton, trimmed to the same size as the other layers.

Over the wadded foundation layers, build up layers of translucent fabrics of any size and shape. Suitable fabrics include nets, lace, organdie, nylon or silk organza. Make as many layers as desired. The pieces of fabric may overlap each other and may be placed at any angle on the background fabric. The final layer should be in one piece, the full size of the background fabric. As an aid in holding odd, assorted bits of fabric in place, a very light application of spray glue may be used. The piece may be hand basted if glue is not used.

When all the layers of fabric are basted together they will be stiff enough to allow free machining without a frame.

Threads Outline shapes with machine embroidery threads in a coordinated range of colours. Select some hand embroidery threads, such as 6-stranded perlé, crochet cotton and wool, to use for cable stitch.

Stitches Use free running stitch and free cable stitch.

Machining Select shapes on the piece to outline with free running stitch. These shapes should be kept simple and should not be too large. It is much easier to work small areas than very large ones. Use your hands to frame small areas while machining.

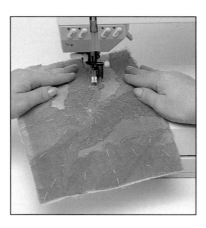

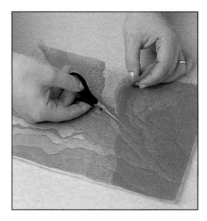

1 Position and layer a selection of fabrics on the background fabric. Beginning at the centre and working out to the edges, baste all of the layers together, by hand.

2 Outline various shapes on the surface of the fabric in free running stitch. Use your hands to hold and frame small areas while stitching.

3 As each shape is outlined, use small, sharp scissors to cut away layers of fabric from within the outline. As the work progresses and you cut out shapes, consider the overall design and colour impact.

Cutwork

As shapes are outlined, use small sharp scissors to cut away layers contained within the outlined shapes. The number of layers cut will determine the colour and texture of the exposed areas. As the work proceeds, and as bright colours and pleasant textures are exposed, you will develop confidence in selecting which layers to reveal.

Free cable stitch The next stage is to edge the shapes with free cable stitching, remembering to work with the back up. Take care to follow the pattern areas outlined in free running stitch, and make constant checks to the front to ensure that the design ideas and colours are as desired.

Finish by removing basting threads and edging the work. The choice of edging will be somewhat dictated by the end use of the piece: the edges may be bound, taped, satin stitched or, if the embroidery is to be framed, left as they are.

The numerous layers of fabric, together with the batting, will give the finished piece a beautiful, quilted effect.

4 When all of the shapes have been outlined and the cutwork completed, turn to the back of the piece. The free running stitch applied to the front will be visible on the back. Free cable stitch is then applied, front (right) side down, following the outlines.

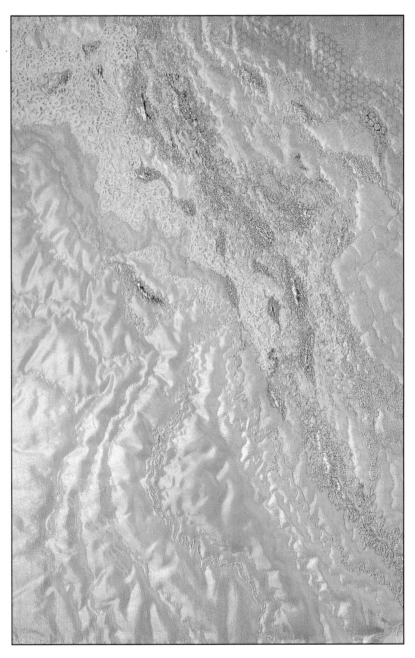

Arctic Blizzard *incorporates the techniques of layering, cutwork, and free machine embroidery stitches. The piece measures approximately 48cm × 63.5cm (19in. × 25in.).*

Creating fabric by machine patchwork

All the colours of the spectrum are present in nature: they all 'go together'. In the same way, all colours will go together in embroidery, it simply depends upon the proportion and placement of the colours. The creation of patterns and colours that blend together well is something of a mystery to many people. To de-mystify these problems, a simple exercise can be done, and the same exercise may be carried out in conjunction with the section on dyeing.

Fabrics Three pieces of fabric of graduated sizes are required. Begin with a square with sides measuring between 7.5cm and 15cm (3in. and 6in.). The second piece must allow a margin of about 5cm (2in.)

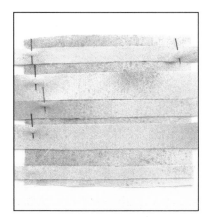 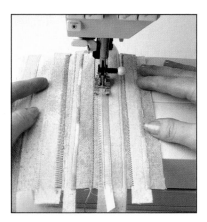 

1 Using a straight edge, pencil some lines of various widths on the smallest piece of fabric. Cut along the lines, making several strips of fabric. Lay these strips, parallel to each other, on the second layer of fabric. The strips should be turned about or alternated to vary the colour layout. Allow part of the background fabric to show between some strips.

2 Using an automatic stitch of your choice, sew the strips to the second layer. The layer may be further enhanced by applying cable stitch, couched hand embroidery threads, cords, ribbons or other materials that will blend with the background.

3 Repeat the first stage, this time drawing lines of varying width *across* the strips applied to the second fabric. Cut the strips, then arrange and pin this new set of strips to the third, and largest, fabric. Re-arrange the strips, playing with them and turning them end to end until the pattern pleases you. The idea is to move and shift colours.

on each side. The third piece should allow a similar margin around the second piece. You may choose to dye your own fabric: if so, refer to page 114 and use a marbling technique to dye the squares. Alternatively, use three different strips of fabric in a small multi-coloured print design with colours that relate to each other. The fabrics will be layered. The smallest piece will be the first layer and may be any medium-weight fabric. The second should be a medium-weight cotton; the final layer – the largest piece – being a medium- to heavy-weight cotton.

Threads Use machine embroidery or dressmakers' threads. Match the threads to the background colours where possible.

Needle Choose a needle to suit the fabrics.

Stitches Use any automatic stitch of your choice. Vary widths while stitching.

Foot Use either the zigzag or straight stitch foot.

Tensions Decrease the top tension slightly, and set the bobbin tension at normal.

Variations

Before the last layer of strips is applied to the background fabric, baste a layer of batting and a covering fabric to the wrong side of the background (largest) fabric. When the embroidered strips are sewn to this piece, the result will be a quilted and embroidered fabric with a sculptured appearance.

Alternatively, follow the instructions through step 2, and then, instead of attaching the strips to the third background fabric, butt the strips together and join them with a decorative automatic stitch. This will result in a piece of decorative fabric that may be used for any purpose.

4 Using automatic stitches, sew the new strips to the largest of the background fabrics. Leave strips of background fabric showing through. An interesting effect may be created if the seams of the strips do not match up. As before, additional threads and materials may be couched or applied.

Stitching in space

Stitching in space is an original technique developed by the author. The aim is to incorporate a preponderance of machine applied threads with a minimum of background fabric. It is also a way of working free machine embroidery without using a frame.

The success of this technique relies on finding a fabric that will support the tensions created when stitching across holes (space) made in the fabric. Some of the fabrics successfully used are combinations of pelmet Vilene and canvas, but it is worth experimenting with other fabrics of similar qualities, to discover whether or not they may be used. Once the basic grid of 10cm (4in.), described here, is mastered, other machine embroidery skills may be used in conjunction with this technique.

Fabrics Use good quality embroidery canvas, with 21 threads to the inch, and pelmet Vilene.

Threads Fine metallic threads give the stitched space a firm quality. Cotton threads work well, as do machine embroidery threads.

When metallic threads are used, only fill the bobbin to about three-quarters of capacity. If your machine does not cope well with metallic thread, try using cotton in the bobbin. Sensitivity to the colours chosen for the top and bobbin can produce beautiful shadings as the threads entwine during stitching. You may experience difficulties when shiny threads are used for this technique.

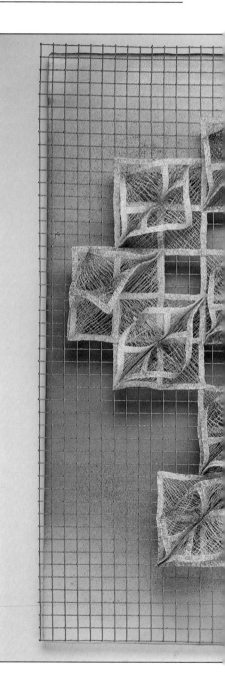

The stitching-in-space technique was used to create this work, Aurora Borealis. *After they were stitched, the squares were then manipulated and stitched to a wire grid. (Embroidery by Gail Harker, borrowed from Mr and Mrs Steve Last.)*

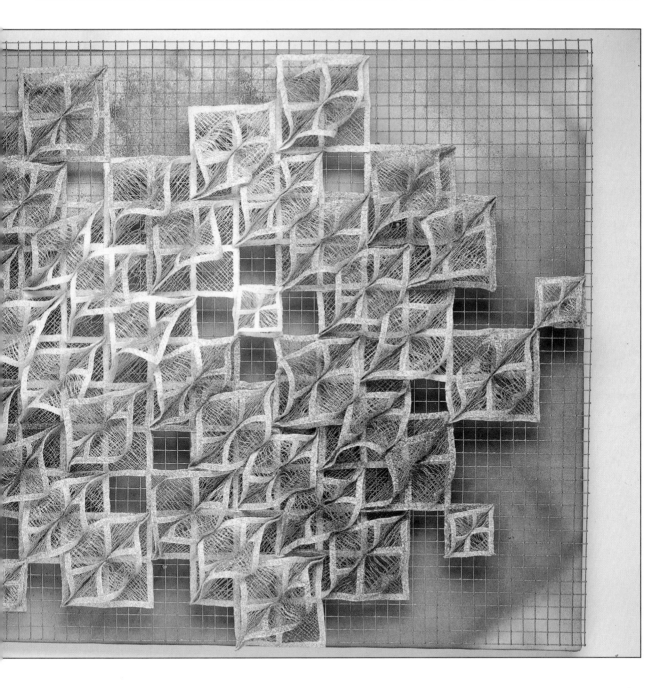

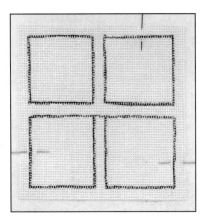  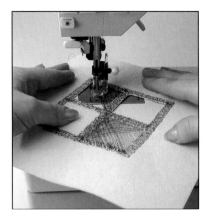

1 Cut the canvas into 10cm (4in.) squares, and the Vilene into 20cm (8in.) squares. With a light application of spray glue, join the two fabrics, leaving a 5cm (2in.) border of Vilene around all sides of the canvas. Draw a frame around the edges of the canvas, with a cross shape in the centre. This will look like a window with four panes. This framework should be between 1cm (½in.) and 5mm (¼in.) in width. For greatest measuring accuracy, count threads.

2 Straightstitch around the edges of the grid, within the 1cm (½in.) framework, to secure the Vilene to the canvas. With very sharp scissors or a craft knife, cut through both fabrics to remove each of the four squares or panes (as if doing cutwork), but remove them one at a time, after stitching has been applied to the preceding square
The resulting grid will be used to support the stitches.

3 Cut away any one of the squares, to prepare for sewing. Start at an outside-middle corner and sew on the spot to secure the thread and build up motor speed. When high speed is attained, cross the open square diagonally to the opposite corner, stitching in space. Repeat the sequence, moving diagonally across the square, toward the outside corner of the grid, until half of the grid is covered with threads. Return to the starting point and repeat the process, moving diagonally toward the centre corner, until the other half of the square is filled in. Following the same sequence of sewing, use straight stitch to crosshatch the first diagonal stitching. Work from the centre corner to the outside corner, stitching diagonally, first in one direction, and then the other.

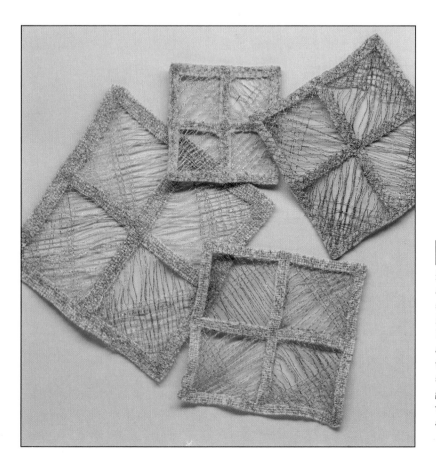

4 Repeat the process, filling the square diagonally opposite the first square stitched. Continue until all the squares have been cut and stitched. Trim away the surplus fabric around the edges of the grid. Free machine embroidery may be added to the framework of the grid, to enhance its appearance or to strengthen the edges. Individual grids may be manipulated into various shapes for special applications.

Needle Use either a 100(16) or 110(18). It is necessary to change needles frequently, because Vilene dulls the points.

Stitch Use free running stitch.

Foot A darning foot is recommended.

Tension Slightly decrease both top and bobbin tensions.

Stitch length Set the stitch length to '0'.

Manipulation of fabrics

Part of the purpose of machine embroidery is to create interest on fabric, or to create interesting fabric. This is achieved through the creative re-making of fabric, using some or many of the techniques described. Often, the very act of making or re-making fabric will suggest an embroidery technique that will work well with it. Try to let your imagination run wild. Consider the properties of the fabric and the ways in which you can turn these to your advantage.

Ask some questions of the materials, such as: will the edges curl when burnt? does the material bubble when burnt? will it fall into soft curves when folded? will it fold into hard edged pleats? will it take dye? can holes be pierced in it? can the edges be frayed?

Burning Some of the synthetics, especially 100 per cent nylon, may be singed without leaving a brown edge. This may be used to create graceful curves and features that will not unravel. Not all fabrics will respond in such a way, and some may burst into flames. Always burn a small sample piece first, taking care to carry out your experiment in a safe place.

Ruching fabric by machine

Ruching is a technique used to manipulate fabric into folds, soft gathers and creases. Stitching across the gathers holds the shape permanently. This is another way of adding texture to embroidery.

Fabric For the background, use any medium-weight fabric. For ruching, use very soft, light-weight fabric, such as satin, silk, muslin or cotton.

Thread Use machine embroidery thread. If the thread is the same colour as the ruched fabric, the stitches will not be conspicuous. Try using invisible nylon thread for the top of the machine. It will blend into any and all fabrics.

Stitches Use either free running stitch on the spot, or free zigzag stitch on the spot.

Foot No foot is needed, but use the darning foot if your machine works better with a foot.

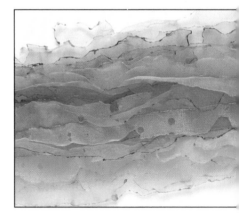

Burning
The seam allowance is on the right side of the fabric. Cut the seam allowance to the desired shape. Using matches, lighter, or other manageable flame, singe the edges of the fabric. This will seal the edges and stop any unravelling. You may also be able to burn controlled holes in the fabric.

Bubbling
The bubble effect on the nylon organza is achieved by holding the fabric some distance from a flame or heat source. Ensure that the fabric does not get too close to an open flame or too hot a heat source, or holes will be made. In this example, two fabric layers were then machined with free running stitch and whip stitch to a background fabric.

Preparation Place the background fabric in a frame. Mark your design on the background, indicating the areas to be filled with ruching. Lay the fabric to be ruched in the marked areas and pull it into small puckers.

Machining Place the frame under the needle and lower the presser bar. Stitch on the spot, using either free running stitch or free zigzag stitch, attaching the applied fabric to the background.

Manipulate the applied fabric with your fingers as stitching progresses. Raise the presser bar to move from place to place over the fabric. Lower the presser bar each time stitches are applied. The threads left between stitches may be left as they are, forming a part of the decoration; they may be clipped close to the stitch, or they may be cut and pulled through to the back of the fabric and tied off.

If it is desirable to have the gathers even smaller and more closely spaced, remove the frame from the machine and finish ruching by hand, using a stab stitch: bring the needle up through the fabric and down very close to the same spot; move the needle under the background fabric to the next position and continue.

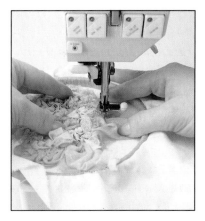

Ruching
Ruching in progress: about 10 stitches are placed on the spot and the frame is then moved to another position. Continue until the design is complete.

95

Ruching with automatic stitching

This technique differs from free machining in that the ruching is laid down in strips. The fabric is pushed together into gathers. Automatic straight stitch or zigzag is applied over the length of the gathered strip with the foot on.

If you want to make the stitching a feature of the piece, parallel rows of stitches may be applied, set very close together over the ruching. If the gathers are to be the main feature, keep the stitching widely spaced.

Fabric For the background, use any medium- to heavy-weight fabric. Use soft, light fabrics for ruching.

Threads Machine embroidery threads, or No. 50 dressmakers' thread.

Stitches Automatic straight or zigzag stitch.

Variation

Heavily starch the ruching fabric, using any starching product (follow manufacturer's instructions). Pinch the fabric into many gathers, and let the material dry naturally. When dry, the fabric will retain the shape. Attach the starched fabric to the background, using the automatic ruching technique already given.

Elastic shirring with automatic stitches

Fabric may be gathered by loading machine elastic in the bobbin and stitching the fabric. The elastic must be stretched slightly as it is loaded on the bobbin, and the bobbin tension should be decreased slightly. Use dressmakers' thread on the top. Very light, thin fabrics will produce soft folds. Use automatic straight or zigzag stitch to create gathers while stitching.

Try gathering a piece of water-soluble lace for use on cuffs or for a textured effect on a panel. To achieve a quilted effect, lay the gathered piece on a background fabric backed by a piece of batting. Add straight or zigzag stitches to attach the gathers, and quilt the piece. A third option is to stitch first in one direction, and follow this with stitches crossing at right angles. This results in an interesting, puckered effect.

Ruching with automatic stitching
Different widths of fabric are laid on the background fabric. The fabric is pulled under the needle and into gathers as you stitch.

Sculpturing fabric

To produce a bubbled effect, mark circles of different sizes on fabric. Using automatic straight stitch with a long stitch length, sew around the circles, leaving long tails on the threads. After stitching around all the circles, pull the top threads on each circle, pulling the circle into a puff. Fill each puff with a little polyester batting, added from behind. Soft, stretchy fabric is particularly suitable for this technique, as are muslin, silk, satin, velvet, jersey or lingerie fabric.

Try some variations on the theme: for example, use a transparent fabric and fill the puffs with pieces of dyed batting; try making bubbles from ruched fabrics, or apply some machine-embroidered stitches within the circles.

Sculpturing fabric
Stitch circles on transparent fabric with a long basting stitch, then pull the threads, gathering the fabric. The circles are then filled with dyed, multicoloured wadding.

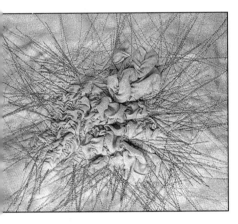

Elastic shirring
Elastic is shirred onto a fabric, which is then laid on a larger piece of fabric. Automatic straight stitches are used to attach the two pieces to each other.

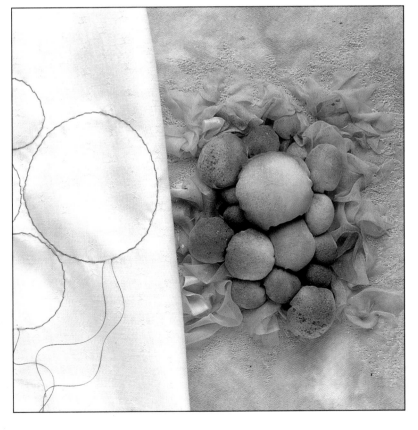

Stitching on paper, plastic and other manmade materials

It is sometimes desirable, to create a particular effect, to stitch on materials other than fabric. Most thin plastic can be stitched, as can most paper products. Handmade papers can be very strong and rigid, and may be used for free machine or automatic stitching. Paper will dull needles, however, so these will need to be changed often. Try bubble packing, plastic wrap or vinyl. It may be necessary to use a roller or teflon foot to smooth progress over these types of material.

Heavy-weight sew-in interfacing may also be used as a fabric for machine embroidery or for use in appliqué. Appliqué is very easy with interfacing: since the fabric does not fray, a single line of stitching is all that is needed to attach pattern pieces. Large banners or children's projects can be produced solely from interfacing, which takes colour very well. Try spraying it with automobile spray enamels or acrylic sprays, but use sprays sparingly – thick appli-

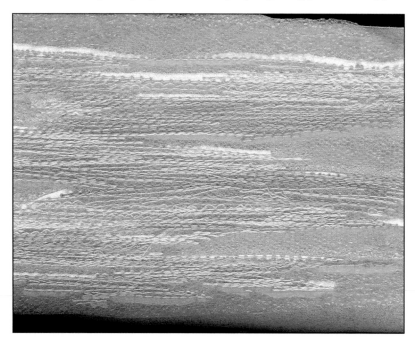

Automatic straight stitch on packing plastic.

cations will stiffen the interfacing. Since fabric dyes do not absorb evenly, a mottled effect may be achieved with dyes.

Pelmet Vilene makes an excellent base for stitching, and because it is so stiff, both automatic and free stitching may be applied without a frame. Satin stitch with machine embroidery threads will give excellent coverage, and you will find that the stiffness allows you to manoeuvre easily, creating graceful satin stitch curves.

Free machining on layers of nylon organza and leather, with a bottom layer of plastic foam.

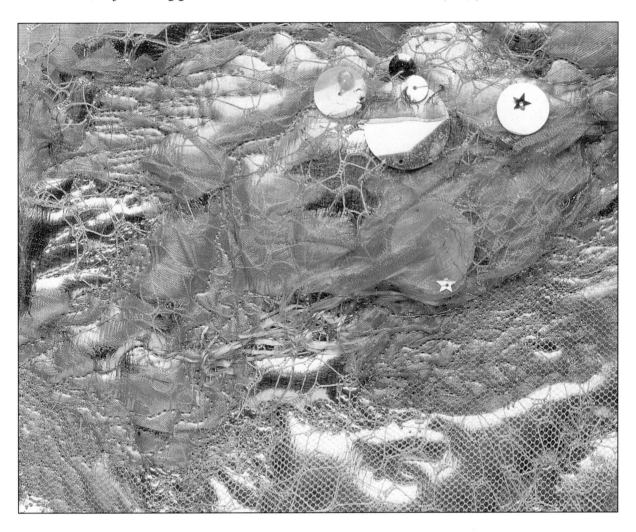

CHAPTER 5

DESIGNING FOR MACHINE EMBROIDERY

One may become, through practice and experiment, a fine technician of machine embroidery stitching techniques. However, unless the stitching is applied to good designs, using good colour coordination, the end result will not be as successful as it could be. This chapter will suggest some design ideas, but it is well, if you have not had the opportunity to develop a good design sense, to refer to any of the numerous, excellent books on design.

Machine embroidery is an art medium, and one ingredient of success in this field is to cultivate your artistic awareness: look at paintings, advertisements and illustrations that catch your eye. Try to analyse why you are attracted to them – it could be a striking blend of colours, a strong focal point that draws the eye, or it could be the subject matter that is of interest.

When developing your own, individual designs, observe contemporary design in fabrics, fashion, floor tiles, magazines and so on. A 1940s design idea, unless it is used for a specific purpose, will look decidedly dated.

The embroiderer without extensive art training may feel intimidated at the prospect of drawing or putting ideas on paper. However, designs for embroidery need not be exact representations of nature or objects. It is sometimes best to isolate a small, interesting area of the subject. If you do this, it may help to make designing much easier.

Some design concepts are more successful than others, and the degree of success depends in part upon the finished product. A repeat design, for example, may be more successful in a garment, tableware or a quilt than as a picture. With a repeat design, there is no centre of interest or focus in the design itself.

The design for this panel of cats peeping through foliage, created by Rosemary Graver, was transferred to the background fabric with transfer dyes. The stitches are free running, free cable and hand running stitches.

Developing designs

Start with an object or theme that is of personal interest. For the writer, Canadian winters have been a source of inspiration. One way of developing that theme is to write word pictures, inspired by poems and stories, of winter. These word pictures will promote many different ways of looking at the world, but it also helps if you collect visual materials, such as postcards, photographs or paintings. It is easy to forget scenes, and the moods that they inspired, so keep a notebook and write down the effect of the seasons or weather conditions on the subject that has caught your attention. Note colours, textures, shapes, and the feelings that they generated.

These exercises should help you to convert observations into graphic representations. Find ways of depicting thoughts and words on paper: try drawing; paint with watercolour or tempera; tear or cut pieces of coloured paper into shapes, and glue them to a sheet of paper – in effect, experiment with any medium that is available, or that is comfortable to use, attempting to convert your ideas into graphic form.

When you have translated your impressions into your chosen medium, look for the segment that is of greatest interest, and isolate that special area by redrawing or tracing it, eliminating all the surroundings. The subject could be a twig, a branch from a tree, or an interesting display of shadow or colour. Try some design ideas from personal photographs, closeup snaps of objects, or magazine layouts. Cut stencils, and stipple or spray areas in colours that are harmonious with the subject. In choosing fabrics, threads or other materials, the aim is to convey the textures, feeling, colours and shapes desired. You might, for example, investigate the possibilities of plastic wrap, bubble-packing material, plastic sheeting or paper. These could be used to create samples of the design ideas that have been generated. In all these experiments, try to capture the colour balance, textures and feeling of the original ideas.

A worksheet for a winter scene, showing sources of inspiration and early samples.

Working on texture of icicles using :— leather plastic quilting trapunto

Shapes icicles

Various shades of thread considered for the cape

Can I trap these feathers between 2 layers of fabric

Nylon Organza has an icy effect if the edges are shaped & singed

One of many samples for cape idea

Glacier Patterns

Repeating shapes

Repeat designs may be used to great effect when you work large pieces of embroidery; for example, the same design may be combined in the same work in enlarged and reduced versions. Quilts, table-cloths, clothing and hangings are all suitable vehicles for the repeating designs described below.

Rectangular repeating designs

Cut a rectangular window from card. Position it over various sections of the source until you find an area that is of interest. Redraw or trace the isolated area on a separate sheet of paper. Make several copies of this area (the quickest way to do this is to use a copying machine). Use tracing paper to create mirror images of the design.

Cut out the isolated shapes and try positioning them in a regular pattern: alternate images; turn them back to front, top to bottom, or mirror image to original, making an arrangement that seems pleasing to the eye. As a further development, treat this arrangement as a single image and make more copies, then try arranging the combined images into a larger composite design.

Circular repeating design

Construct a circle of any size, using a compass. Without changing the compass radius, start at any point on the circle and tick the circle at the two points of intersection. Move the compass to one of the points ticked and make two additional intersecting tick marks. Continue until there are six ticks around the circle. Draw a straight line from the centre of the circle to each of the six ticks. The result is a circular design, with six triangular shapes.

Cut out one of the triangular shapes and use it as a window, as in the previous method. Find an interesting triangular shape on the design source and, as before, trace over the shape. Arrange copies of the tracing into a circle.

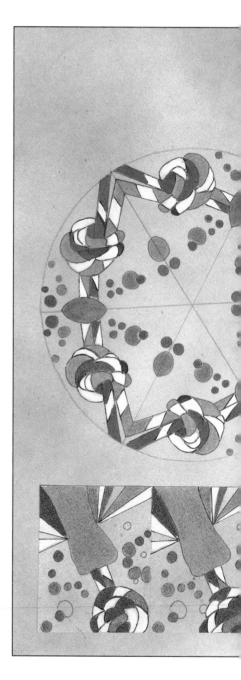

A series of design experiments shows the creation of rectangular and circular repeating designs.

Designs from photographs

Most of us have favourite photographs, either snapshots taken on holidays or studies of subjects that are of special interest to us. Whether you use an existing photograph or take one of a subject that offers design possibilities, the resulting images can be turned into designs.

Select the photograph(s) to be used. Cut a window of any shape – circle, square, rectangle or triangle – that seems appropriate. Using any of the repeating design techniques, isolate the desired section(s) of the photo and simplify the subject matter. Develop the design as in any repeating design technique.

This design by Penny Butterworth originated from a photograph of a culvert pipe. It was simplified and made into a repeat pattern. Reverse appliqué was used with satin stitches and zigzag.

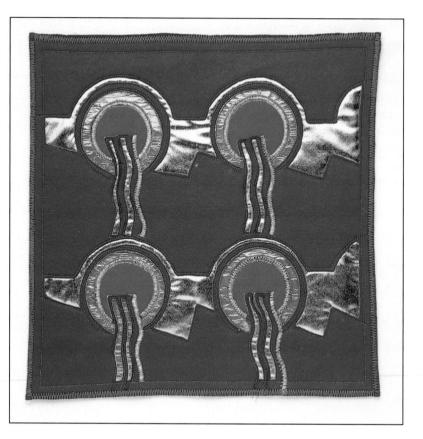

Designing with cut paper shapes

A very simple design method begins with cutting paper into pleasing shapes. It is more exciting to print, spray or dye your own paper for this purpose. These shapes are then arranged into a collage, forming a design. This method is very good when designing for appliqué, fabric creation or quilting.

To begin, select papers in the colours chosen for the design. Cut shapes from the appropriate colours and fit the pieces together, gluing them to a sheet of paper. When you have produced the desired design, with an attractive blend of colours, you can translate it to fabric.

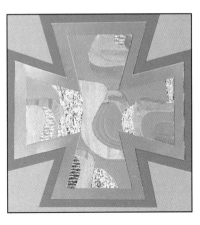

A selection of cut papers were glued to a background paper to create a design idea for an ecclesiastical embroidery. To make the finished embroidery, Beryl Tucker basted six layers of fabric together. The design was traced on paper interfacing, which was placed over the fabric layers, and all the design lines were machined. The interfacing was torn away, and the appropriate layers of fabric were carefully cut away. Handmade cords were couched in close satin stitch along the design lines.

107

Creating texture with threads

Wonderful textural and sculptured effects are possible with machine embroidery. It can be difficult, when viewing an array of machine embroidery threads in the store displays, to visualize the effect they will produce. It is only when the threads are stitched alongside each other that the differences can be readily seen. Texture and dimension can be produced through the use of thick and thin threads, along with mat and shiny finishes.

Experiment is the obvious route to developing a vocabulary of thread and stitch techniques. Try a selection of stitches and various machine tensions on a number of threads: the resulting samples will indicate when and where a thread/stitch technique may be used in the work. Experiment with as many stitch techniques as possible, in order to discover the range of textures that may be produced. Using various threads/stitches, work on unusual fabrics and papers. Create your own fabric, using the techniques described, and add threads and stitches for extra texture and interest.

In a way, it is like learning a foreign language – you need to develop a vocabulary before putting it to useful application.

More texture

Machine embroidery is a medium that can allow a considerable interaction between the stitches and the background fabric. As a result, the relationship between threads and background fabric is critical. Choose a fabric that will work well with the selected technique and threads. Machine embroidery can appear very flat, but this will be more than offset when special techniques are used.

The following checklist gives some of the techniques that can lend additional texture and depth to a machine embroidery:

> quilting, patchwork, trapunto, dyeing, italian cording, fabric layering, fabric manipulation, appliqué, reverse appliqué and hand embroidery.

All of the above are described in detail in other chapters.

Used skilfully, these will result in added height, depth and texture.

Fabrics were layered and then decorated with a wide range of threads to create the wintery feel of Ice Angels.

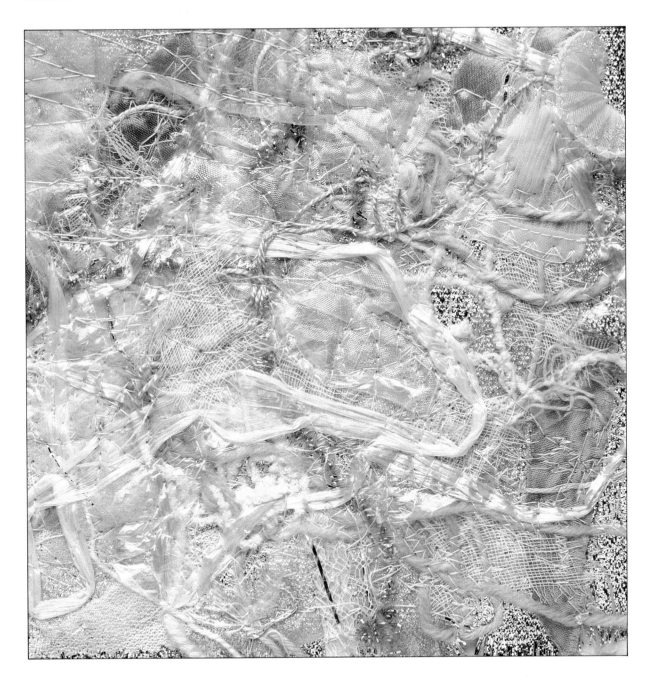

Colour

We are continually stimulated through our visual senses: light and colour flow in at us from every aspect. Our emotions are roused in predictable ways through colour; some of that stimulation being learned, and some being instinctive. Marketing experts use research into the psychology of colour to select package colours: to incite us to buy products, they wrap the goods in colours that we associate – positively – with the product on offer.

Through the ages, we have been conditioned to react to certain colours, but our colour reactions vary from culture to culture. For instance, in western cultures, black is associated with mourning or sadness, while white indicates happiness, purity and weddings. In the orient, the reverse is true: white is the colour denoting mourning and sadness.

Red is most often the colour used to impart anger, hate, fire and danger. Blue signals peace and coolness. We all react to colour, and it is therefore important for a machine embroidery artist to have an understanding of colour and to know how to make it work positively.

The mix of colour

A colour can look very different, according to whether it is viewed in isolation or displayed alongside another colour. Our eyes are the colour blenders. We have long known that the three primary colours will produce the whole colour spectrum. Using the primary colours, and our eyes to mix them, we are able to see a full range of colour produced by our colour television sets, though the screens only show red, green and blue dots. Colour printing, as seen on post cards and magazines, relies on the same principles. With a magnifying glass, one can see the printed dots of primary colour, plus black for shading.

These principles are also available to the embroiderer. The mix of coloured threads and fabrics is comparable to the mixing of colour on a painter's palette. The many variations in tone of thread and fabric provide an infinite variety for the embroidery artist. It is as important to the embroiderer as it is to the painter to be aware of and to plan colour for every composition.

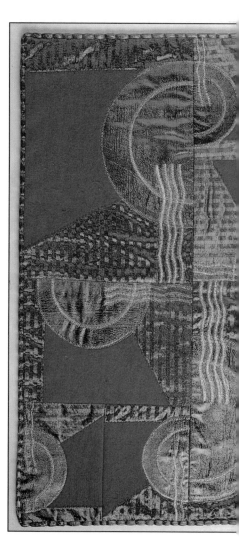

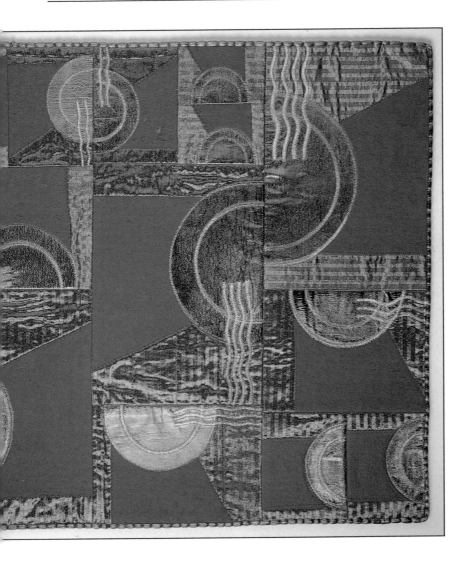

Penny Butterworth used appliqué and zigzag stitch to make this panel. At one time, it was thought that blue and green should not be put side by side, but if the proportions and tones are well chosen, the mixture can look stunning.

Colour proportion

We owe much to the artists who have preceded us and, collectively, spent many lifetimes studying colour. A visit to any art gallery will graphically illustrate a massive range of colour combinations. Look carefully at a few paintings: observe the amount used of any one hue and tint, compared to all the other colours in the composition – in other words, the colour proportion.

As an interesting exercise, you might produce a colour proportion chart of a favourite work. The chart will be of valuable assistance in understanding colour proportion and balance, when you come to design your own works.

Colour proportion chart

To make a colour proportion chart, take an elongated rectangle of white paper or cardboard. While carefully studying a painting, attempt to isolate and duplicate the colours and tones observed. Estimate the amount of each colour or tone present. Apply each colour to the rectangle in approximately the same proportion as it is present in the source. When all of the colours have been applied, the chart is complete.

It is useful to have a supply of hand painted papers to use for design. This is one way of discovering what interesting colours will look like when juxtaposed.

The colour proportion chart may be used to create an embroidery using the same colour proportions, and the resulting work should be as pleasing to the eye as the source.

Fear of colour

If you study the works of both old and modern masters, you will find that all those so-called 'rules' for mixing colours have long since been rejected. A look at the variety and beauty of the colours of nature will immediately show that there are no rules. This small fact should release anyone from the fear of making incorrect choices while experimenting with colours. Feel free to do as the spirit moves you.

Colour in machine embroidery

High contrast between thread and fabric is not necessarily an advantage. In fact, contrasts, such as black on white, can look very cartoon-like and lacking in depth. It is generally much more effective to use colours that harmonize with the background. A single colour in one area can also look very flat, so it is better to use a number of threads of closely matched shades. Variegated threads can also add a feeling of dimension.

This colour proportion chart by Rosemary Graver was used as a basis for the panel on page 101.

Marbling with a paint brush

Most fabrics must be prepared for dyeing, though some fabric is sold ready to dye. If your chosen fabric is not prepared for dyeing, or if there is any uncertainty, start by washing it in water with detergent. Cottons may be washed in fairly hot water, but silks and wools require cooler water and mild detergents. The purpose of the washing is to remove any sizing or factory-applied finishes from the fabric, as this may interfere with absorption of the dye.

Considerable personal experimentation with dyeing techniques has led to one method that is reasonably fast, easy to accomplish, and provides colour-fast fabric.

This method, which creates a marbled fabric, entails the use of a paint brush to apply dye. In this way, a useful length of marbled fabric can be produced in one batch.

Deka silk dyes are used for the process. These dyes will work on silk, silk substitutes (synthetics) and most cottons.

To begin, lay sheets of plastic over the work surface. Wet the fabric, then wring out excess water and lay the fabric over the plastic sheeting. Deka silk dye colours, when prepared to the manufacturer's instructions, are very intense, but softer shades may be achieved by diluting the dye in water. Simply add water to the dyes until you have the desired colour.

Using a 5 to 10cm (2 to 4in.) paint brush, apply the dye to the fabric. Several colours may be applied. Keep a laundry spray (atomizer) nearby to spray the fabric with water if it dries. Cotton, in particular, has a tendency to dry before all the dye is applied, and this inhibits the spread of the dye.

After applying dye, you can give the fabric a mottled effect by sprinkling salt over it while it is still wet.

Allow the fabric to dry naturally. Depending upon the weight of the fabric, this could take from one to three days.

Whatever dye you use, ensure that you follow the manufacturer's instructions when you fix the dye. Deka silk may be fixed by ironing the fabric with a hot, dry iron, but do not attempt to fix the dye until the fabric is dry. It is quite easy to dye five or six metres of fabric at a time with this method.

The silk fabric has been laid on plastic sheeting and painted with an ordinary household paintbrush.

Textural effects with dye on fabric

You can sometimes stimulate your imagination by printing or dyeing your fabric first, rather than beginning to embroider on a plain piece of fabric. Many attractive designs can be made by using everyday objects such as dye stamps, to create interest on fabrics. The following is just a selection from the numerous possibilities.

- Thread reels/spools
- Sponges of varying textures
- Toothbrush – for spattered effects
- Corks
- Potatoes – halved and with designs cut in relief from the flat sides
- Wood blocks
- Crumpled fabrics – net, tweed, knits and so on
- Pipe cleaners – bent into various shapes
- Rope or string
- Nail heads – in blocks
- Paint brushes

Any type of fabric may be used as long as it will accept the dye. Try Deka Permanent, Pebeo Seta Color or Dylon Paint On, but experiment with other dyes, bearing in mind that the dyes must be tacky, not runny.

To protect the work surface, a sheet of plastic should be laid over it before you start the dye process.

The background fabric may already have been given an all-over dye to your own specification, or it might be a piece of coloured fabric. After laying down the background fabric, daub, poke, paint, roll, spatter, brush or in almost any other fashion apply a design. For a runny effect, water may be sprayed over the design.

Dry the dyed material naturally or use a hair dryer to speed up the drying process. Fix the dyed fabric with a hot, dry iron to make it washable and dry-cleanable, placing a pressing cloth both under and over the dyed fabric while ironing. It is best to check the manufacturer's instructions before fixing the dye.

1 Silk fabric is 'sponged' with paint-on dye. Cut shaped holes in the fabric to prepare for machine embroidery.

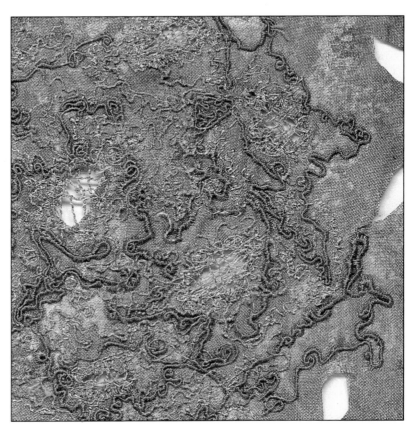

2 Apply whip stitch, following the flow of the dye. Work free running stitch over the holes to create a lacy filling.

Transferring designs to fabric

There are no hard and fast rules for the transfer of designs to fabrics. Different fabrics, and also different embroidery techniques, may demand particular methods of design transfer. Some pieces of work may require a very accurate transfer of design, but others may not.

Some of the free machining techniques require no design transfer at all: in this style of embroidery, the needle can sometimes be used as pencil to draw the design in stitches, directly on the fabric.

Prick and pounce

One of the oldest systems for the transfer of design is the prick and pounce method. This is used where a design must be transferred very accurately to a fine textured fabric. The method is not, generally, satisfactory for rough textured or piled fabric.

Draw the design on tracing paper. Fix a fine needle – 60(8) or 65(9) – in the machine, but do not thread the machine. Set the stitch

Prick and pounce

 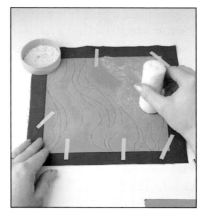 

1 After pricking the pattern by machine, lay the pattern on the fabric. Ensure that the pattern does not move as the powder is applied or the lines will be smudged. Pin, tape or baste the pattern to the fabric.

2 Dip the end of the rolled pad into the pounce powder. Gently rub the powdered end of the pad over the pricked lines in the paper.

3 Carefully lift the paper from the fabric. Using a very fine brush, paint over the lines of powder with fabric dyes recommended on page 116.

length slightly shorter than is usual for straight stitch. With the feed dogs up and the general sewing presser foot down, stitch over the design lines. Make only one pass over each line. The result will be a paper pattern, pricked with fine, regularly spaced holes.

Make a pounce by taking a piece of felt or other soft fabric, about 10cm (4in.) wide, and rolling it into a pad of about 3cm (1¼in.) in diameter. Stitch it to prevent it from unrolling.

Different powders should be used, depending on whether or not the fabrics are light or dark in colour. If special pounce powder is not available (check with your art supply shop), powdered charcoal, powdered cuttlefish bone, French chalk or talcum powder may be used. You will also need a fine paint brush and fabric dyes.

Design transfer with transfer paint

Transfer paints are also known as iron-on transfers. They are very easy to use and are produced in many colours. First paint your design on drawing paper, using as many colours as desired. When the paint is dry, lay the paper with the painted surface on the side of the fabric that is to receive the transfer. Lay a second sheet of paper over the transfer paper, and, with a very hot, dry iron, press the transfer area, following the manufacturer's instructions. This will produce washable and dry-cleanable fabric. The same paper transfer can be used to produce four or five prints on fabric, although the colour may become reduced towards the end.

Transferring designs with stencils

Stencils are most successfully used with medium- to heavy-weight fabrics. Cut designs from stiff cardboard or stencil paper, using a sharp craft knife. Double-sided tape may be used to fix the stencil to the fabric, after which the dye can be applied with a stencil brush or an air brush, or you might use a toothbrush to spatter selected areas. After the dye is dry, it may be fixed according to manufacturer's instructions.

Stencils may also be made with a low tack plastic sheeting, available from art suppliers. The design is cut, as above, and the film is then removed from the backing and stuck to the fabric. The advantage of this film is that it is transparent.

Transferring with paper interfacing

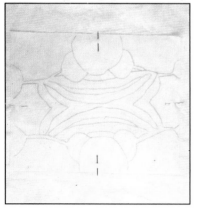

1 | Draw a design on paper interfacing. Place it over the fabric, face up, and pin it in position. If desired, the fabric may be framed.

2 | With the general sewing foot on, stitch around the design, using straight running stitch. Use normal or slightly shorter than normal stitch length. Free machining may be used, if desired.

Transferring a design to the back of the fabric

The application of the design to the wrong side of the fabric is especially useful for appliqué. Start by basting together two fabrics of the same size: one will serve as the background fabric; the other is the appliqué fabric.

Draw the design on a sheet of tracing paper. Turn the paper over and pin it to the back of the background fabric. This is done to ensure that the image is not reversed on the right side of the fabric. Stitch along the design with automatic straight stitch, piercing the paper and fabrics. This will transfer the design to the fabrics. After all design lines have been stitched, tear away the paper.

Turn the fabrics to the right side and cut away any excess fabric around the appliqué design. Finish the appliqué from the front (right) side, using free machine or automatic stitches.

Transferring cable stitch design

When designing for cable stitch, the design may be drawn on the wrong side of the fabric, except, of course, if the fabric is transparent. Since cable stitch is worked from the back of the fabric, the design will be easy to follow and none of the design lines will show.

Backlit design transfer

Draw the design in very dark felt-tip pen or pencil on light-weight paper, then position the fabric over the paper and shine light through both.

Unless you have a lightbox, the window is likely to be the most convenient light source. Simply tape the design to the window; position the fabric over the design, and tape it to the window. The design may then be clearly seen through the fabric, allowing it to be traced with a tailors' marking pencil or a very hard drawing pencil. If, however, the lines are likely to show through the finished stitching, use dotted lines to reduce the amount of visible pencil.

Photocopy transfers

The development of the modern photocopier has provided embroiderers with yet another method of producing transferable designs and patterns. To transfer a design from the copy paper, make a solvent of one part water to one part white spirit (paint thinner). Add about a teaspoon of liquid detergent.

Protect your working surface with several layers of fabric. Lay the photocopy, print side up, on the surface. With a large watercolour brush, quickly paint the solvent over the surface of the photocopy – a light coating will be sufficient.

Position the fabric (light cotton works best) over the photocopy. Apply a light coat of solvent over the transfer fabric until it adheres to the copy. Do not apply too much solvent – the material must not be sopping wet. Place a few layers of fabric or paper over the transfer fabric, and press with a dry iron set to the hottest temperature. Do not let the hot iron come into contact with any solvent. This method is best used to provide an outline pattern over which dyeing or embroidery techniques can be applied. The transfers are not washable, because the inks are not fast and will run.

Finishing techniques

After a precious and unique piece of embroidery is completed, the question of how to finish it off arises. If a wall hanging is to be the end product, the piece may need to be stretched and framed, though some wall hangings are more attractive without neatly finished edges. The finishing of the work may be every bit as important as the work itself. There are many approaches to finishing off embroideries, and it is only possible to discuss a selection of the most useful and effective methods.

Soft hangings

Soft hangings may have special characteristics, such as folds, creases, movement or a free form. Such designs cannot effectively be stretched over frames, but are better allowed to hang loosely from the top. If the shape is intended to be a precise rectangle, it is important to measure accurately and check that the sides are absolutely parallel and corners are square.

To ensure that soft hangings are properly supported and hang as they are intended, they will need to be lined. The lining fabric will protect the back of the work from dust and other environmental effects, and will also give it a neater appearance. The lining could be made from curtain lining or a fabric similar to one used in the work. Be sure that the grain of the fabrics (embroidery background, interlining – if used – and lining) all run in the same direction, or the embroidery may not hang straight.

Interlining may also be used to provide additional weight, to pad the work, and to facilitate the finishing. The interlining may be a soft fabric such as flannelette, cotton, blanket material or other, similar, non-stretching fabric. Interlining, however, is optional and can be omitted if it will serve no useful purpose.

Some options

Some large embroideries, due to the delicate nature of the materials, may not hang correctly. This condition can be corrected by adding drapery weights to the fold at the bottom of the main fabric before you attach the interlining.

1 Cut interlining to the size and shape of the finished piece. Let the embroidery overhang the interlining by about 3cm (1¼in.) to allow the edge to be turned without adding excess thickness. Fold the interlining back to the centre of the work. Starting at the fold, working to the bottom, secure it to the work with a lockstitch at 30cm (12in.) intervals. Repeat on the other half of the interlining.

2 Fold the edges of the embroidery over the interlining and pin it in place. If the embroidery is not too bulky, the corners may be mitred. Otherwise, fold the edge of the embroidery over the interlining and secure with a herringbone stitch, continuing along each side in the same way.

3 Cut the lining material, leaving an overhang of about 1cm (¼in.) around all edges of the interlined work. Measure down from the top of the lining, about 3cm (1¼in.), and draw a line. Along this line, on the finished side of the lining, machine stitch the top edge of the furry side of 2-sided Velcro tape. Cut the tape slightly shorter than the width of the work. Be sure to allow enough lining material to turn under, retaining a small margin between the top of the Velcro and top of the work.

4 Turn under and baste the edges of the lining, then position the lining on the back of the work. Baste one side of the Velcro in place along the top edge, then lockstitch the top and bottom edges of the Velcro to the interlining. Some of the stitches should go through the interlining and show on the front of the work. Continue lockstitching the remainder of the lining to the interlining. Slipstitch the turned edges of the lining to the interlining. Fix the other side of the Velcro to a strip of wood, using tacks or a staple gun. Attach the wood strip to the wall and press the embroidery in place, using the Velcro strip.

Embroideries need not be rectangles or other regular shapes – some very successful pieces are free and irregular in outline. Edges need not be finished and this may add to the tactile nature of the work.

Embroideries may be hung from wooden poles or other hanging devices. Flat pieces may be mounted on cardboard, perhaps framed with a card mount, and displayed in commercially available frames. Some frames may not require any mounting of the embroidery.

Troubleshooting your sewing machine

People normally expect their machine to last a lifetime. Most will. But none will last long and give good service without proper maintenance. Regular brushing – to remove fluff and lint from in and around the bobbin case and under the needle plate – is essential. Machine embroidery will produce more fluff and lint than will conventional sewing, and therefore demands that you pay more attention to maintenance.

Some newer machines are self lubricating, but many are not. Again, machine embroidery will create a need for regular oiling, so always check the manual for your machine for oiling instructions. This is necessary because one machine will differ from another. Take great care, however: too much oil may stain fabrics, and machine parts need only be moistened with the oil.

To be a successful machine embroiderer, it is essential to be able to find and correct some of the oft-occurring troublesome problems. You can identify many faults and correct them without technical training and without having to stop work to take your machine to the repairer. The following is a guide to finding and correcting some common troubles.

TROUBLE	REMEDY
Top thread does not pick up bobbin thread	The needle may be inserted back to front or not inserted high enough into the needle slot. Check your machine manual.
Skipped stitches	Fabric may need to be tightened in the embroidery frame.
	Synthetic fibres are often the culprit with skipped stitches: try natural fabric or use a special ballpoint needle for sewing synthetic fabrics.
	The needle may be dull, bent or damaged. If so, change it.
	The needles may not be correct for your machine: check the manual for the system number.
	Ensure that the top of the machine is properly threaded, check your manual.
	Try using a darning foot for free machine embroidery.
	Check to see if the needle plate is bent or nicked. Often, if the needle has broken on contact with the needle plate, the plate can be bent, nicked or damaged. This will interfere with proper sewing.

Top thread breaks or shreds	The needle being used may not be of sufficient size to allow movement through the fabric without shredding the thread. Try a larger needle.
	Could be very old thread.
	The needle may be damaged or bent.
	The fabric may need to be tightened in the embroidery frame.
	When using certain special embroidery threads, it is sometimes advisable to bypass the thread guide immediately preceding the needle. Ensure that the top of the machine is otherwise properly threaded.
	Check to make sure that the bobbin is the correct one for the machine in which it is being used.
Thread spools off the reel, twists itself up and breaks	Add an extra thread guide beside or behind the top reel holder and slightly higher. It is possible to improvise by taping a large-eyed darning needle to the machine. Bernina and Elna produce an attachment for this purpose which fits on the reel holder.
Bobbin thread breaks	Check to ensure that the bobbin tension is not too tight.
	The bobbin may not be wound evenly.
	Thread may be wound over the rim of the bobbin.
Thread keeps tangling	Ensure that the presser bar is down while you are sewing.
	The top thread should be threaded while the presser bar is in the up position.
	The top tension may be too tight to allow the top thread to pass between the tension discs as it is being threaded.
	Ensure that the bobbin case is properly inserted. Check your manual.
Thread looping under fabric	Check to ensure that the hole in the needle plate is correctly aligned with the needle in the centre of the hole.
	Ensure that the presser bar is in the down position while you are sewing.
	The bobbin tension may be too tight.
	The top thread tension may be too loose.
Noise in machine	The hook and race may need oil: check the manual.
	The race may be clogged with lint. Brush it out before oiling.

General hint   It is always good practice to give the race a good brush-out
– often – and to keep the mechanical parts of the machine clean.

INDEX

ACKNOWLEDGMENT

I should like to thank all the embroiderers who kindly lent their work for inclusion in this book. In addition, I should also like to thank the following: Pfaff (Britain) Ltd – for the loan of sewing machines, needles, and accessories, and for useful information; Frister and Rossman Sewing Machines Ltd, for the loan of a sewing machine; Elna Sewing Machines (G.B.) Ltd – for the loan of a sewing machine; Fraudenberg Nonwovens Ltd – for interfacings; Madeira Threads (UK) Ltd – for threads and soluble fabrics; A. West & Partners Ltd – for Pebeo fabric paints and dyes, and Morris and Ingram (London) Ltd – a touch up gun for use with fabric paints.

Note: All work is by the author unless otherwise credited.